THE **WHARNCLIFFE COMPANION** TO

NOTTINGHAM

Boundary marker, dating from 1933.

THE **WHARNCLIFFE COMPANION** TO

NOTTINGHAM

AN **A** TO **Z** OF LOCAL HISTORY

GEOFFREY OLDFIELD

Wharncliffe Books

First published in Great Britain in 2005 by
Wharncliffe Books
an imprint of
Pen & Sword Books Ltd
47 Church Street
Barnsley
South Yorkshire
S70 2AS

ISBN 1-903425-70-0

A CIP catalogue record for this book is
available from the British Library

Typeset in 10/11.5pt Plantin by Mac Style Ltd, Scarborough, N. Yorkshire
Printed and bound in England by
CPI UK

Pen & Sword Books Ltd incorporates the Imprints of Pen & Sword Aviation,
Pen & Sword Maritime, Pen & Sword Military, Wharncliffe Books, Pen &
Sword Select, Pen and Sword Military Classics and Leo Cooper.

For a complete list of Wharncliffe titles, please contact
Wharncliffe Books Limited
47 Church Street, Barnsley, South Yorkshire, S70 2AS, England
E-mail: enquiries@pen-and-sword.co.uk
Website: www.wharncliffebooks.co.uk

Contents

Nottingham Canal is now a popular leisure resource, as can be seen in this photograph, near London Road, showing anglers on a sunny day.

Preface

Nottingham has been a place of residence for about 1,500 years. In writing this account, the greatest difficulty was therefore in deciding what to leave out. I hope that readers will not be disappointed if they do not find a mention of something they would like to see. I can only suggest that they refer to some of the many other references to the City's history that exist. I have not included a bibliography of some of the many sources which I have used. The reason for this is that there is now available *A Nottingham Bibliography*, published by the Thoroton Society of Nottinghamshire in 2002. This was compiled by Michael Brook and lists publications on Nottinghamshire history before 1998. This comprehensive work runs to 420 pages and has references to 8,707 publications. Of those, 2,520 refer exclusively to Nottingham itself. The remainder includes 1,984 items devoted to Nottinghamshire, which does include references where appropriate which relate to the whole County, including the City. A comprehensive 'places' section includes those separate places which combine to make up the City.

In the years since 1998 there have been many new works on Nottinghamshire history. These can usually be found in Nottinghamshire public libraries, as well as in the university libraries, and private ones such as Bromley House. Details of most of these recent works are usually given as reviews in the twice-yearly issues of the *Nottinghamshire Historian* and the annual *East Midlands Bulletin of Local History*. Newsletters of local history and similar societies often have references to new and recent publications.

I would like to thank Mr John Croome for permission to include the photograph on page 153 which remains his copyright. The remaining illustrations are either from my own camera (and copyright) or picture collection.

I would also like to thank Mrs Irene Young for typing the manuscript with infinite patience.

The clock tower is all that remains of Nottingham's former Victoria railway station. The Victoria Centre flats are on the right.

Introduction

The earliest written mention of Nottingham occurs in AD 868 when the Danish army took up its winter quarters in the Anglo-Saxon *burh*, or borough. Archaeological evidence points to its having been founded two or three hundred years earlier, on a strategic small cliff site overlooking the Trent Valley. In the ninth century it became one of five towns of the Danelaw and important as part the administration of a central part of England.

As an English borough, after the integration of the former kingdoms, Nottingham increased in importance and royal favour, with its own mint and a bridge over the River Trent which helped communications southwards. When the Normans came to Nottingham in 1068, they built a primitive castle which later became a royal palace. This was within the new borough, which the French built round the castle and the earlier Anglo-Saxon borough to the east became known as the English borough.

The two boroughs eventually merged to become a mercantile, trading and manufacturing town as well as the market centre of the immediate agricultural region. Its importance can be judged from the number of its royal charters, especially two which permitted it to have a mayor, and even more importantly, created the town as a corporate body, separate from the jurisdiction of the county.

The post-medieval period was influenced as elsewhere in the country by the political turmoil of the Stuart regime. The civil wars resulted in the town becoming strategically involved in the early years of the conflict. The end of the seventeenth century saw a revival of Nottingham's fortunes, following the stabilisation of the constitutional and religious problems.

Two developments which helped this revival were the beginnings of a textile industry in the East Midlands based on the stocking frame and the building of a ducal mansion on the site of the former castle. The eighteenth century saw a gradual transformation of parts of the town, with the re-building of larger houses for gentry. Nottingham became known as a pleasant town with gardens and orchards, but this was largely to disappear in the second half of the century. The population tripled in this period to a figure of 29,000 in what became an increasingly overcrowded industrial town, due to the refusal of the burgesses to allow expansion of the town on the surrounding former common fields.

This was only overcome at the end of the first half of the nineteenth century, which had seen the decline of hand-wrought hosiery industry, off-set by the increasingly mechanised lace industry. It was also a period of reform of out-moded forms of local government and gradual recognition of the worst social and environmental features.

The second half of the nineteenth century saw Nottingham becoming the centre of the country's lace trade and also further industrial growth in other trades, particularly engineering, cycle manufacture, tobacco and pharmaceuticals which were to become vital in the next century when lace declined. This period also saw the extension of the borough boundaries to take in surrounding villages, its creation as one of the first county boroughs and the granting of city status in 1897. The population of a quarter of a million in 1901 was not far short of what it is today, although the city area has increased from 10,000 to 18,000 acres.

The twentieth century, as elsewhere, saw a first half largely influenced by two world wars. Nottingham did, however, use the period between 1919 and 1939 to make considerable progress modernising what was still largely a Victorian city. The second half, like that of the second half of the previous century, saw vast changes in transport, the demolition and rebuilding of mainly working class houses, the flight of older manufacturing industries accompanied by new sectors of financial services, along with cultural, entertainment and educational changes. In the last two decades and into the twenty-first century, the greatest transformation has taken place, and is continuing to do so, within walking distance from the city's ancient market place and its dominant Council House.

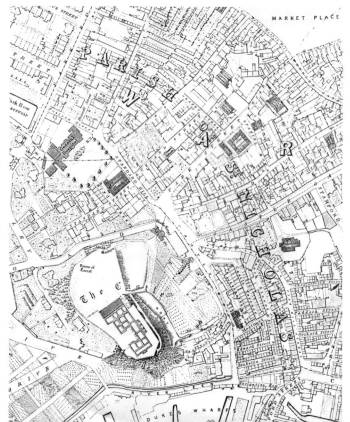

Nottingham Castle and its environs, from a map published in 1861.

The Wharncliffe Companion to Nottingham

ABATTOIR

Nottingham's abattoir, adjoining the Cattle Market on Meadow Lane, was purpose-built for the slaughter of animals. It was opened in 1939 and was the first such public building, replacing a practice of several hundred years duration of using slaughterhouses by butchers, often adjoining their shops. In 1797 Quarter Sessions granted to Robert Parr a licence to operate a slaughterhouse on Butt Dyke (Park Row) for slaughtering any horse, mare, gelding, colt, filly, ass, mule, bull or cow, heifer, calf, sheep, hog, goat or other cattle which were not killed for butcher's meat.

During the nineteenth century the Council considered the state of slaughterhouses, especially after a government inspector commented on the existence of pig sties and slaughterhouses adjoining houses, 'with accumulations of blood and refuse and cesspools all sending out noxious effluvia' (bad smells!). In 1859 the Sanitary Committee recommended that a separate range of slaughterhouses be built to replace the existing fifty-three.In 1899 the Butchers' Association protested against the Council erecting public abattoirs, but the local branch of the RSPCA was in favour of them.

In the 1930s it was still possible to see herds of cows in the streets causing timid old ladies to seek refuge in doorways and shops.

ACADEMIES

White's Directory for 1832 gives a list of eighty-five educational establishments under the heading 'Academies'. Most of these merely give the name and address of the persons running them. Many of the latter were women whose standards of teaching led to them usually being called, derisively, 'dame schools'. The directory gave more information about the others in a separate article headed 'charity schools'. These were classified into twelve categories with a total number of pupils of 1984. These included three, which had been formed earlier than the nineteenth century. The oldest was the Free Grammar School for boys from 1513, the Blue Coat of 1706 for boys and girls and the Unitarian, 1789, with sixty-four boys and girls. All three are still in existence in somewhat modified forms.

The largest of the other schools were the National for 550 and the Lancasterian, with two schools, one of 220 boys and the other for 100 girls. These were part of national systems set up in 1808 and 1811. The Lancasterians, named after its founder, Joseph Lancaster, were later known as British Schools, the Nationals being supported by the Anglican Church.

Goodacre's Standard Hill Academy was there from 1807 to 1891 and was reputed to be the best private school in Nottingham.

The directory also described the new Charity School in Barker Gate attached to the Salem Independent Chapel. This was founded by two men who noticed that several hundred children of the poorest parents could not attend Sabbath Schools because of lack of decent clothing. This led them to run about the streets, 'imbibing the germs of idleness and sin'.

There were also four infants' schools conducted on 'an ingenious system by which infants between the ages of two and six were under a pleasing interchange of exercise, amusement and instruction. They experienced a gradual development of their bodily and mental powers'.

AFFRAYS

'An attack or assault' is how today's dictionary defines 'affray'. In 1395–6 some forty affrays were recorded during the mayoralty of John de Plumtree. The wording is usually the same in each case, apart from the names of the decennaries, the complainant and the attacker. The decennaries were men for each ward of the town who acted as constables. The affrays were described as 'with blood' or 'without blood' and defendants were usually fined amounts varying between six pennies and twelve pennies.

Stephen Wade was said to have beaten Agnes Irish and drawn blood, against the peace of our Lord and King etc. – and was fined six-pennies.

A rather more serious view was taken when William Bunche, messenger of the Sheriff of Nottingham, was attacked by Thomas Fox, draper, who lay in wait for him, and beat him, wounding him with force and arms. He was fined six shillings and eight pennies. This would have been a considerable sum in those days, but the Court seems to have had regard to the means of miscreants. Maud, the wife of John Boyn, 'from her own will and motive threw down and beat Agnes de Lenton with her fists'. She was led away to the Common Hall by the Mayor's bailiff where she 'broke the key of the Hall and took herself away from thence without the licence of the Mayor and bailiffs'. However, she was 'forgiven because she is poor'.

AIR RAID PRECAUTIONS

Unlike the First World War, which came as a shock to most people, the second one was subject to much speculation in the late 1930s as to whether or when war would break out.

Events in Spain had revealed the nature of modern aerial warfare and particularly after September 1938, when 'peace in our time' was said to have been obtained, action was taken to try to prepare the civil population to deal with war on the 'home front'. The Government had passed instructions to local authorities, especially on the possibility of the use of poison gas. Gas masks were delivered to the civilian population of Nottingham before the war. Other signs of activity were in evidence. Army searchlight and anti-aircraft units were set up and the City Council appointed an Air Raid Precautions Committee. Work was started on building air raid shelters and on strengthening basements of buildings. Preparations were made for setting up an air raid warden service, for fire watching and for emergency action in the event of their necessity. The worth of these precautions was justified by subsequent events.

AIR RAIDS

Britain did not have air raids during the 1914–18 War to the same extent as it did in that of 1939–45. It did experience some attacks by airships, known as Zeppelins, the inventor of them being a German count of that name. Nottingham suffered one such attack in January 1916 when a number of buildings were damaged. These were mainly in the area around Greyfriar Gate and Broad Marsh and some took place to the south of the Midland Station. There were few casualties. Street and other lights were not 'blacked out' all the time, but only on the receipt of a warning of an attack.

The Mayor of Nottingham complained to the Home Office that the staff at the Midland Station did not put lights out, a factor which the Mayor said led to the bombs falling where they did.

The Second World War saw continuous and heavy bombing, particularly in London, and targets such as ports. Nottingham did have several small raids during the war, but the major attack was on the night of 8/9 May 1941. The raid took place on a bright moonlight night so the River Trent showed up clearly. Targets were on both sides of the river, at Sneinton and West Bridgford. One of the most devastating incidents was a direct hit on a bakery on Meadow Lane, where people were working on the nightshift. Many people were killed there and some bodies were never recovered or identified. A special section of graves with appropriate memorial stones was provided in the Southern Cemetery. Other buildings damaged in the city centre included the Moot Hall on Friar Lane, the Masonic building on Goldsmith Street and the west wing of University College, as it then was, on Shakespeare Street. Both the latter two buildings were successfully repaired after the war.

This plaque is on the wall of what was then Boot's headquarters on Station Street (now occupied by Capital One).

After the raid on Nottingham a large number of bombs fell on rural areas around the Vale of Belvoir. It was said later that this raid too was intended for Nottingham but the defence system was able to alter the navigational beam used by the German aircraft.

ALABASTER

One of the skilled trades of medieval Nottingham was the making of sculptures from alabaster, a mineral of which a large deposit was at Chellaston, Derbyshire, conveniently near to the Nottingham workshops. The name of one of these craftsmen was Nicholas Goodman, whose name appears in a list of licence fees paid in 1479 by various tradesmen. He was described as 'alebasterer' and paid eight pennies.

Nicholas Pevsner in his Nottinghamshire volume of *The Buildings of England* (1951) said there are twenty pre-Reformation alabaster figures in the county's churches. Most of these are in Holy Trinity Church, Ratcliffe-on-Soar, as monuments to the Sacheverell family. Other examples were sent to other counties and to Europe.

ALBERT HALL

The foundation stone of the first Albert Hall was laid on 1 September 1873. It was named after the late Prince Consort and opened three years later, on 26 September, by the Mayor of Nottingham, John Manning. It had been designed by Watson Fothergill and cost £13,000. It had been erected by a company and a prospectus advertising shares modestly claimed that its size, form and internal appearance would make it the finest concert hall in the Midland counties.

The opening ceremony was followed by a performance of Handel's *Messiah* although the performance was marred by the noise of stone chipping outside the building. The hall was to be used for other purposes than concerts including, in 1895, Louis Tussaud's exhibition 'All the World in Wax' and in the same year a Chamber of Horrors with a collection of torture instruments. The Wiertz Gallery of Replicas of the extraordinary works of the mad Belgian painter was another exhibition.

The building was destroyed by fire in April 1906 having been bought four years earlier as a Wesleyan Methodist Mission. It was rebuilt in 1909 to a design by A E Lambert who also designed the two main Nottingham railway stations. It became the main public hall and was used in addition to its Methodist Mission for concerts and other events. Two well-known annual events were the Music Festival and the November Chrysanthemum show. Movable seats were replaced by fixed ones, which restricted its use for the latter. The larger symphony orchestras also found its facilities inadequate and would not play there. The building of the new concert hall on the site of the former Empire Music Hall no doubt influenced the Methodist Mission to amalgamate with the Parliament Street Methodist Church and sell the Albert Hall to the City Council. It is now run by the Council in much the same way as the original building.

The Albert Hall, designed by architect Watson Fothergill, burned down in 1906 and was later re-built.

ALDERMEN

In the Charter of 1449 granted by King Henry the Sixth, it proclaimed that the Mayor and Burgesses of the town were to be an incorporated community. In addition they could appoint from among themselves seven Aldermen, one of whom was always to be Mayor. In addition the seven Aldermen were to be the seven Justices of the Peace or Magistrates. The Aldermen so appointed were to remain as such for their lifetime unless they were removed from office by the Mayor and Burgesses for 'any notable cause' or by their own special request.

In time the Mayor and Aldermen appointed men, who had to be Burgesses, to offices such as Chamberlain, Sheriff and Bridgewardens. These were usually for one year and the custom gradually evolved whereby such Burgesses were

Aldermen were in great demand for laying foundation stones and other ceremonial duties. Alderman John Barber is seen here in 1869 helping to lay a memorial stone to celebrate the start of building the new Trent Bridge.

placed on a list known as the 'Clothing' and it was from this list that new Aldermen were elected when one died. This undemocratic process, which applied equally to other Charter boroughs, led to a call from early nineteenth century reformers for the system to be altered. This was eventually achieved by a Municipal Reform Act in 1835. This provided for Councillors to be elected by ballot, and for Aldermen to be elected by the Councillors from amongst themselves or from persons who were eligible to be elected as Councillors. The number of Aldermen was to be one sixth of the number of Councillors.

In practice most Aldermen who were elected for a term of six years, were chosen from Councillors, apart from one or two occasions. Richard Birkin and Lewis Heymann were two nineteenth century Aldermen who were never elected as Councillors. They were chosen because of their experience as successful businessmen.

In 1974 when local government was re-organised, the office of Alderman was abolished. Nottingham, as a District Council and now a Unitary Authority, has appointed honorary Aldermen, former Councillors with long service. Their duties are mainly ceremonial and they do not take part in running the Council.

ALEHOUSES

Before tea and coffee became generally available ale was regarded as necessary to drink as bread was to eat. The Mayor of Nottingham held 'Assizes of Bread and Ale' at which the price of the two commodities was regulated. Ale and beer at one time were practically synonymous but beer later became the name for darker ale, after English soldiers in the wars against France discovered the practice of using hops to flavour the drink.

Whilst it was common practice to brew one's own ale, alehouses were popular for more social reasons. As early as 1463, the burgesses passed an ordinance or by-law against 'Ale-houses receiving suspicious persons, or keeping their houses open after nine of the clock'. In 1467, Elizabeth Wright, described as a 'common scold', was fined six pennies 'for holding a common tavern about the middle of the night.'

In the early nineteenth century, the drinking of gin and other spirits became so widespread that the Government passed a Beer House Act in 1830. This provided that householders might sell beer, but not spirits, on payment of two guineas. Alehouses had to be licensed by magistrates.

Nottingham ale had a reputation for strength as evidenced by a popular song, *Nottingham Ale Boys, Nottingham Ale.*

☛ *See also Brewing*

ALLOTMENTS

Before 1835, under the old unreformed Corporation, the term 'allotment' meant the perquisite enjoyed by some of the burgesses.

If the sign on the wall of the Trip to Jerusalem *is true, it must be the oldest alehouse in Nottingham.*

This consisted of a lease of corporate land at a modest rent for the burgess to use. They could either use it themselves for growing crops or grazing or could rent it out to someone else.

After 1835 when this custom ceased the term 'Allotment' in Nottingham became used in much the same way as it is today. The economic conditions of the town at that time were such that there was a wide variation in living standards. Skilled men and those with staple trades were reasonably well paid by the standards of the time. Most of the rest of the population suffered extreme poverty from time to time. Because of the changes of fashion in the hosiery and lace trades, and the cyclical economic stress, any unemployment affected the workers and there were no alternative sources of employment. In the absence of any form of financial assistance, apart from poor relief, some efforts were made to alleviate the situation. One such method was the provision of gardens or allotments for those out of work. The aim was to provide food for the men and their families and to avoid the hated new poor law which pauperised its recipients.

A man who played a considerable part in organising such efforts was the Reverend James Orange, who was not only a non-conformist preacher but also a businessman and a historian producing his *History of Nottingham* in 1840. He campaigned for a Cottage Garden Society, to provide homes for working-class families with gardens. He was of course not alone in this aim and the Corporation, which after the Enclosure Act of 1845 had land available, played its part by establishing allotments. A large tract of land known as Hunger Hills was used for this purpose and by 1853 it was estimated that there were over 5,000 allotments in and around Nottingham.

These 'whilst fulfilling a primary purpose of supplying cheap food' also had a recreational value. The St Ann's allotments became famous for their roses and until the 1960s an annual St Ann's Rose Show was held on the Arboretum.

The Corporation's Estates Committee had an allotments sub-committee, which included members from the garden holders' associations. As Nottingham expanded, some of the allotments succumbed to the need for providing sites for houses. In more recent years the demand for allotments diminished as other leisure activities arose. However, more recently, when an allotment site at Bulwell was needed for industrial purposes, the holders protested and the Council has provided new allotments nearby.

ALMSHOUSES

The earliest almshouses, then known as hospitals, were founded by wealthy persons for the care of the poor and elderly. The earliest reference is dated between 1162 and 1174 in a document from King Henry II confirming a grant of land. The rules of one of them, St John's Hospital, have survived which include an order that the men and women were not to visit each other in the night except in cases of illness. As the hospitals were administered by the church, they were suppressed in the same way as other religious houses by Henry VIII.

In 1390 John Plumtree founded a charity to provide accommodation for poor widows. The original almshouse was re-built in 1824 and the building in Fisher Gate still stands, now let for commercial use. The tenants were re-housed in 1968 to new accommodation in nearby Canal Street. These dwellings have now been demolished.

Numerous other almshouses were erected, especially from the eighteenth century onwards. Their sites in the city centre became valuable in recent years and the proceeds of their sale were used to build new modern houses in the suburbs.

AMATEUR PHOTOGRAPHY

Following the introduction of professional photography in Nottingham a number of talented enthusiasts took up the hobby of photography particularly as a means of artistic expression. They soon formed a society through which they could exchange experiences and hold exhibitions. The Nottingham

The foundation stone of the Plumtree Almshouses was laid by the Mayor in 1823.

Photographic Society, formed in 1858, ceased activities in 1860 mainly due to technical difficulties affecting outdoor photography. Later developments in processing and cameras helped to establish a new society in 1884, Nottinghamshire Photographic Association, which later changed its name to reflect its status, to the Nottinghamshire Amateur Photographic Association. When this body ceased in 1892, a new organisation, a Camera Club was set-up by Nottingham Mechanics' Institute. This body, in addition to organising talks and exhibitions, carried out a photographic survey of places in the county. It later became the Nottingham and Nottinghamshire Photographic Society, which still flourishes today.

Nottingham was fortunate in having two talented amateur photographers whose work was recognised internationally. Both had successful careers, Samuel Bourne (1834–1912), established a large textile firm and Arthur Marshall (1858–1915) the architect who designed what became Nottingham City Hospital as well as other major buildings.

☞ *See also Photography*

APPRENTICES

The custom of apprenticeship of boys to a particular trade was important to Nottingham from medieval times. This was recognised by the fact that the practice was formalised by a legal agreement, drawn up and witnessed. This required the master and the apprentice to act for a period of years as teacher and pupil, at the end of which term the pupil became a qualified tradesman or journeyman. This system ensured that the town had a constant supply of craftsmen, with the advantage to the master of a cheap assistant and to the apprentice an assured qualification. This was seen by the Corporation as vital to the town's economy by regulating the system which had a secondary importance as a successfully completed apprenticeship was one way of the man becoming one of the select body of the town, the burgesses. [☞ **see Burgesses**]

An early example of an apprenticeship agreement or indenture was entered into on the 24 October 1488 between Robert Parleby and Hugh Smyth of Nottingham, barker (tanner) for six years, Robert receiving sixteen pennies a year for five years and thirteen shillings and four pennies for the last year. It was witnessed by the Mayor and the two Sheriffs.

In 1562 an Act of Parliament made it unlawful for anyone to set up in trade or manual occupation unless they had served an apprenticeship for at least seven years. On 3 December 1578 Thomas Nix was summoned at the Mayor's Court and fined £22 for having traded as an ironmonger without having been apprenticed.

This seems to have led the following March to the Common Council making an order that all apprentices should bring their indentures to be enrolled.

ARCHITECTS

The earliest record of an architect designing a Nottingham building would appear to be on an inscription tablet in St Leonard's Church at Wollaton. This refers to the work of Robert Smythson who designed Wollaton Hall (with a little help from the owner, Sir Frances Willoughby). Smythson is described as 'Architector' and 'Surveyor'.

In 1725 the Council decided to build a new Guildhall in the Market Place. The Mayor, Alderman Marmaduke Pennell, was appointed surveyor of the building and was 'desired to prepare a plan of the said Building and present it to the Hall with what speed he can.'

The building became known as 'The Exchange' and Marmaduke Pennell can be regarded not only as the architect, but as a competent one, as the building remained in use for two hundred years. It was demolished to provide the site for the present Council House.

Pigot and Company's Directory for 1828–29 gives a list of trades and professions in Nottingham, which includes five names under

Watson Fothergill who changed his name from Fothergill Watson. He became one of Nottingham's eminent nineteenth century architects.

Fothergill often 'signed' his buildings in the way he did at his own office in George Street.

the heading 'architects'. One of these was Henry Moses Wood. He became an Alderman in the reformed Corporation and in 1837 was made Borough Surveyor. He designed a Greek Doric temple style lodge on the main walk of Nottingham Forest, which is still there.

White's Directory for 1853 had a similar list of trades to that of 1829, under 'Architects and Surveyors' with nineteen names. As well as Henry Moses Wood, the list includes Thomas C Hine. He was to become one of Nottingham's most prominent architects. He designed the lace warehouses for Richard Birkin and Thomas Adams, as well being the architect for the Park Estate and for the restoration of Nottingham Castle.

In 1862 an Architectural Association was formed, reflecting the growth of Nottingham, which was to take place from thereon. By 1915 *Wright's Directory* listed forty-six architects and surveyors. A notable feature by that date was the inclusion of a number of partnerships of two or three names. Also included was that of Fothergill Watson, who later changed his name to Watson Fothergill. He rivalled T C Hine as one of Nottingham's most important architects of nineteenth/twentieth century. Biographies of both have been written by K D G Brand for the Nottingham Civic Society.

The Architects' Association became a branch of the Royal Institute of British Architects. One of the most prominent architects of the early twentieth century was T Cecil Howitt. He was Nottingham's Housing Architect when council housing became a major activity from 1919 and he also designed Nottingham's Council House.

ARCHIVES

Records of the Borough and City of Nottingham are held in Nottinghamshire Archives on Wilford Street. These date back to the twelfth century and include minutes, deeds, reports and other documents, not only those of the pre-1835 Charter corporation and its successors, but others from many

Known as Nottinghamshire County Records Office, this building on High Pavement was formerly the Judges' Lodgings. New purpose-built accommodation on Wilford Street is known now as Nottinghamshire Archives.

sources. The vast majority of these are open to inspection. They are housed in a modern purpose-built office opened in 1997.

Some City archives are also held at the University of Nottingham's manuscripts department in the Hallward Library. The library also has an East Midlands Collection of books covering four East Midland Counties.

ART GALLERIES

In 1843 a Government School of Design was established in Nottingham to train workers in trades where skill in design was necessary. Primarily intended for those responsible for lace, provision was also made for watchmakers, printers, engravers and stonemasons. The School was eventually moved to Waverley Street as the School (later College) of Art. A School of Art and Exhibition Committee was set-up and in 1872 an exhibition was inaugurated, which was visited by over 130,000 people. All the exhibits were lent including some from South Kensington and there was a collection of oil and watercolour paintings by a local artist Andrew MacCallum, R A. This was followed by a comment from the committee that the interest shown

> *clearly indicates that the working-classes are become more imbued with a taste for the fine arts.*

This no doubt led to the Council restoring the ruined Castle to form its first Museum and Art Gallery.

Over the subsequent years, the Art Gallery has been augmented by thousands of paintings, prints and engravings, only a small selection of which are on show at any given time. Special and travelling exhibitions are occasionally held.

The City now has two other public art galleries, one of which is in the same building as the Central Library. The other is at Highfields in the Angear Building erected on the site of the former open-air swimming pool. Both galleries have exhibitions of art, which do not usually cover the same type of exhibits as those at the Castle.

ARTISTS

In 1977 David Phillips and Ann Gunn published *Nottingham Castle. The Art A List*. This was the first what the authors called a remotely complete list of Nottingham Art Collections. It is in two sections – 'Paintings, Drawings and Prints' and 'Sculpture'. The latter consists of only one and a half pages covering the work of thirty-two individual sculptors and examples of various Schools. Only in one or two cases do they relate specifically to Nottingham.

The paintings, drawings and prints section runs to seventy-six pages and there are about 1,000 names of artists. The following are some of the artists who had a particular connection with Nottingham either because they were born, lived or work here or specialised in depicting local scenes and have more than one work in the collection:

Bonington, Richard, Senior (1768–1834), five works. Father of the next.

Bonington, Richard Parkes (1802–1828). Born at Arnold but lived in Nottingham for a time. 135 works, mainly drawings and engravings, mostly of European scenes.

Brown, Sir John Arnesby (1866–1955), ten paintings including two local scenes. Has many works in other galleries.

Browne, Tom (1872–1910), eighteen drawings, mainly humorous – illustrator for magazines.

Dawson, Henry (1811–1878), one hundred drawings and paintings with a number of Nottingham scenes and events.

Knight, Harold (1874–1961) and Knight, Laura (née Johnson, 1877–1970), both former students at Nottingham School of Art. Harold represented by nineteen oils and drawings, mainly life studies. Dame Laura by eighteen drawings, engravings and a few pictures. She was famous for her circus and ballet paintings.

Dame Laura Knight's plaque is on a house in Noel Street where she lived at one time, with her husband Harold Knight, also an artist. She was one of the leading painters of the twentieth century.

Oscroft, Samuel W (1829–1913), forty watercolours, mainly of local scenes.

Sandby, Paul (1725–1809) and brother Thomas (1721–1798). Both were born in Nottingham but moved to London in their twenties where they enjoyed royal patronage. The Castle has about 250 examples of Paul's work, especially engravings. Thomas is represented by ten drawings and engravings, mainly of local scenes.

Hammond, Thomas William (1884–1935), has only two works in the Castle, but his works are probably known by more people than many of the other local artists. This is due to a production of a volume in 1926, *Nottingham Past and Present* where fifty reproductions of his crayon drawings are displayed, and, more recently, *City in the Making*, published as part of the celebration of Nottingham's centenary as a City. This has reproductions of fifty-nine of his works which were shown in a special exhibition. In addition, his works have been seen by visitors to the City's Council House and the County's County Hall both of which have some of his works on display.

A more extensive account of *Artists and Sculptors of Nottingham and Nottinghamshire 1750–1950* is by Henry C Hall, published 1953. An account of the work of the first hundred years of the Nottingham Society of Artists is *For the Very Joy of Art* by M McMillan.

ASPLEY

The name Aspley occurs as early as 1108 when it was spelled Aspeleia derived from Anglo-Saxon words meaning 'Aspen-tree clearing'. It was part

Built on one of the 1920s council estates. Aspley, this footpath was formerly the track of a mineral railway line.

of Radford and so became part of the borough of Nottingham in 1877. It was a small hamlet about a mile from the main part of Radford and formed part of a large estate owned by Lord Middleton. The main building there was Aspley Hall, which was demolished in 1928.

When Nottingham started to build council houses, from 1919, it was found by experience that to build economically a sufficiently large area of land was required. By 1928 the Council found itself short of such sites and purchased an area of 290 acres. This was situated on the west side of Nuthall Road and partly within the City boundary and partly outside. A scheme for building 1,200 houses on the part within the City became the first phase of what was then called the Aspley Lane estate. The cost per house was £317. The layout was similar to other estates, with twelve houses to the acre and with only minor roads apart from those on the boundaries. Further houses were later built on the land outside the then City boundary.

ASSEMBLY ROOMS
The increased gentrification of Nottingham in the eighteenth century led to the construction of the Assembly Rooms on Low Pavement. Abigail Gawthern, in her diary, describes the social occasions of dancing, card playing and polite conversation, which took place there. The classical façade remains untouched, the building has been used as a post office until the 1990s and is now combined with the adjoining Marks and Spencer's store.

ASSIZE OF BREAD
The price of bread in medieval times was judged to be of such importance that an assize of bread controlled the price that the bakers could charge. A committee consisting of the Mayor, the two bailiffs and several other 'trustworthy men' met periodically to do this. On 10 October 1395 evidence was given that in the previous Saturday market, the best corn was eleven pennies, the middle quality ten pennies and the poorer quality nine pennies. The bakers were told that they could charge three shillings and six pennies, presumably for a standard loaf.

On 19 December, the prices of each quality of corn had fallen by one penny. The bakers were then told to lower their price to three shillings. The Assize also accused individual bakers of selling bread at prices higher than that fixed by giving short weight. William Brekpot, baker, was found wanting in his weight in a loaf of white tourt bread of a farthing by the weight of five shillings and four pennies. He placed himself in the favour of the Mayor and placed himself in 'misericordea', asking for mercy. He was forgiven by the Mayor because he was poor.

ASYLUMS

In less sensitive times, provision for the care of mentally ill people was referred to as taking place in lunatic asylums. One such example was that for the borough and county, opened in 1812 off Carlton Road in Sneinton. A directory for 1832 stated that an Act of Parliament required that all 'pauper lunatics and dangerous idiots' had to be placed in asylums such as those, the cost being met out of poor rates.

A more appropriately named 'Lunatic Hospital' was opened in 1859 on Mapperley Hills, later called Ransom Road. This was described as being:

> *intended for the treatment and care of persons of the middle class, of limited means, suffering from insanity who though not paupers were unable to pay the whole expense of their maintenance.*

DUKE OF DEVONSHIRE

This Public House has for many years been known locally as
" THE MADHOUSE "
This nick-name originated at the time when patients from the GENERAL LUNATIC ASYLUM, originally sited on Dakeyne Street opposite, were allowed out to visit families and friends and also to visit the original public house built on this site.
The Lunatic Asylum was opened on 12th February 1812, the total cost being £21,000. Accommodation in 1816 was provided for a total 84 men and women.
Part of the Asylum wall is still to be seen at the top end of Dakeyne Street.

This sign is on the wall of the Duke of Devonshire *public house on Carlton Road.*

The increasing population of the borough in the second half of the nineteenth century was accompanied by the opening of the Borough Lunatic Asylum in 1880. This was on a large site between Wells Road and Porchester Road owned by the Borough. The asylum was administered by nine trustees or visitors, appointed annually by the Borough Council. A new wing was added in 1889, bringing the accommodation to 580 patients. After the Borough was made a City, the asylum was called the City Lunatic Asylum until 1920 when it became the City Mental Hospital. When the National Health Service was set up in 1948, both institutions came under Nottingham Number Three Hospital Management Committee as Mapperley Hospital and Coppice Hospital. The subsequent national decision to transfer patients to the community resulted in the Coppice Hospital being converted to residential accommodation, whilst Mapperley Hospital was gradually reduced in size and status.

ATTORNEYS

In 1828–29 *Pigot and Company's National Commercial Directory* was published, one volume dealing with four Midland counties including Nottinghamshire. For the town of Nottingham it listed the principal trades and professions. This included thirty-eight names of attorneys, as solicitors were then known, illustrating the commercial growth of the town. Amongst the names was that of Henry Enfield, who was also Town Clerk. The Enfield family had a remarkable record of being Town Clerks of Nottingham. Richard became the Town Clerk in 1790 but died a year later. His brother Henry became Town Clerk in 1815, after his partner, George Coldham, Town Clerk since 1791, was killed in an accident. Henry served as Town Clerk until he died in 1845, when his son William was appointed as his successor. He resigned the office in 1870 when it was decided that Nottingham needed a full-time Town Clerk.

Another name was William Cursham. His family too provided solicitors in Nottingham for over 150 years, the last one being a partner in the firm Sir Bernard Wright and Cursham.

A rather more exotically named attorney in the list was Caractacus D'Aubigney Shilton, who in a lawsuit against the Corporation was described by the Mayor and another Alderman as one who all his life busied himself as a righter of wrongs – 'though not having the very high esteem of anybody is wonderfully well satisfied with himself'.

BAGTHORPE

In 1883 the Borough Council was looking for a site on which to build an infectious diseases hospital. Approaches were made to the War Office to acquire land on Bagthorpe Hill. Sanderson's map, published in 1835, shows a large house with grounds called Bagthorpe House, on an elevated site near the present prison on Perry Road. The Council eventually purchased a site of 126 acres, being the whole of the glebe land belonging to the Vicar of Basford. The hospital was opened in 1893 on twenty-four acres of the land, at the junction of what is today Hucknall Road and Valley Road.

In 1895 the Estates Committee of the Council was asked by the Board of Guardians if it would make available land adjoining the Isolation Hospital for a new workhouse. The existing workhouse was to be demolished to provide the site for the new Great Central Railway and Victoria Station. This was objected to by the Government's Local Government Board on the grounds that smallpox might spread from the hospital to the workhouse inmates. This did not prevent the workhouse being built as the Council agreed not to treat smallpox cases at the Hospital. The workhouse and infirmary were capable of accommodating 1,700 people.

From April 1930 Boards of Guardians were abolished and their duties transferred to local Councils. In Nottingham, a Public Assistance Committee was set up to administer the Poor Law duties and the workhouse was re-named the City Institution. The Health Committee was responsible for the City Infirmary and the Isolation Hospital.

Under legislation of 1948, the Poor Law system was abolished and responsibility for the relief of poverty transferred to a government body. At the same time responsibility for hospitals was transferred to Regional Hospital Boards and Hospital Management Committees. This resulted for a time for two new names to be given to parts of the Hucknall Road complex, Sherwood Hospital and Heathfield Hospital. These have now changed again and a vast new City Hospital with some new buildings has emerged. It was however some time before the citizens of Nottingham stopped referring to 'Baggie'.

BAILEY, THOMAS AND BAILEY, PHILIP JAMES

Had Thomas Bailey been born in the twentieth century, he would surely have been visited by Michael Aspel with a big red book. He was a man of many parts. He was born in Nottingham in 1785 and in his early days was engaged in the silk trade. In *White's Directory* for 1832 he was described as a wine merchant living in Wheeler Gate. In January 1836 he was elected as a Councillor on the reformed Town Council, a position he held for six years. He had been an unsuccessful Parliamentary candidate in 1830. He played a prominent part in the campaign for the reform of Parliament, so much so that the inhabitants of Basford, where he went to live, erected an obelisk with a plaque on it in recognition of his efforts. This was in the grounds of Basford House, a listed eighteenth century building, which still exists, but was later moved to a burial ground opposite the house. Unfortunately the obelisk has been broken.

In 1845 he became the proprietor of a weekly newspaper, the *Nottingham Mercury*. This had been started in 1825 but when Bailey took over the circulation fell immediately and the paper ceased in 1852. Its lack of success was attributed by one contemporary newspaper to Bailey himself who, it said, 'was everything by turns and nothing for very long'. The closing of the paper did enable him to publish in 1856 his *Annals of Nottinghamshire*, a massive work of 1,758 pages. He also wrote thirteen other works including hand-books to Nottingham Castle and Newstead Abbey as well as some poetry.

He said that his greatest honour was to have been the father of Philip James Bailey, whose poem *Festus*, which was written between 1836–39, was added to over the next fifty years, resulting in a book of 800 pages and 40,000 lines. It is mainly philosophical and theological and it used to be the proud boast of literati that they had read the whole of it. It is best remembered by the following lines:

We live in deeds, not years: in thoughts, not breaths:
In feelings: not in figures on a dial.
We should count time by heartthrobs. He most lives,
Who thinks most, feels the noblest, acts the best.

Philip is remembered by a Holbrook bequest plaque attached to a wall on Middle Pavement next to the site where his house stood. Thomas has a street named after him at Basford.

BAILIFFS

In the year 1283–84, King Edward I in a royal Charter granted the town of Nottingham the right to appoint annually a Mayor from amongst themselves. At the same time they were to appoint two bailiffs. One was for one borough and the other for the other. These two boroughs reflected the dual nature of the government of the town since the Normans built their castle. The part near the castle became known as the French, whilst the other one centred in the old Anglo-Saxon settlement was the English Borough. The two bailiffs were needed 'on account of the diversity of customs existing in the boroughs'.

An interesting sidelight on the circumstances of the town occurred in Letters Patent issued by King Edward III. This was in reply to a plea by the town that in one of the boroughs, on account of the poverty and insufficiency of the inhabitants, they were unable to find anyone to take on the office of bailiff. The King therefore allowed them to elect both bailiffs in whichever part of the town seemed expedient. We are not told which part was the poorer one.

The bailiffs' duties are not set out, but some details occur from time to time, which illustrate some of them. In 1389, Alan Chapman was sued by the late bailiffs for five shillings and four pennies, being a fine which he owed for having drawn blood of Richard Percator. He had been ordered by the bailiffs to wait in the Hall of Pleas until he paid. He did not do so but left the town and 'concealed himself'. He denied drawing blood and said he would not pay and asked that an enquiry as to the truth be made. No further details were recorded.

In 1395, a similar case was reported and this referred to what was a custom of the town that the bailiffs could take the doors from a house if the rent was not paid. Hugh Spicer had had four doors removed for non-payment of rent for a tenement in Castle Gate.

The bailiffs were allowed to have a sub-bailiff. In 1351 Nicholas de Oure was appointed as a sub-bailiff, but was accused of misbehaviour. He was said by the bailiffs to have left their service without permission and gone to London to work for others. He was committed to gaol for his sins.

In the important Charter of 1449 from King Henry VI, Nottingham was granted freedom from all jurisdiction of the county. The Charter also said that the town should have two Sheriffs instead of two Bailiffs.

BALL FAMILY OF LENTON

In the Census Return of 1871 George Ball, aged forty-eight, was living at Willoughby Street, Lenton, with his wife and five children. His occupation was plumber and glazier. Two of his sons were Frederick, aged ten, and Albert Ball, aged seven. Even the most prescient fortune-teller would not have foretold that these two boys would become Aldermen on the City Council, would serve as Mayors and would have successful careers and that one would be knighted. Even more unlikely would have been that one of them would have a son who by some unforeseen miracle would fly through the air, in a machine that no one then could visualise.

Frederick, the elder of the two, became an architect and specialised in designing City schools. He was elected as a Councillor, became Sheriff and later, in 1913, Mayor and an Alderman a year later. He died quite young, in 1915, aged fifty-four. In his Will he had an estate of £31,000.

Albert started his career in the offices of Manlove and Elliott, engineers, but became a land agent and property developer. Elected as a councillor in 1899, he too became an Alderman, and Mayor in 1912. In 1920 he was again elected as Mayor when the current Mayor resigned due to ill health. In 1936 he was made Lord Mayor, which became the title of Nottingham's chief citizen from 1928. He died in 1946, aged eighty-two, having served on the City Council for forty-seven years.

Sir Albert became one of the City's most influential members of the Council, and was for many years Chairman of the Gas Committee. His

This statue in the Castle grounds is to Albert Ball, VC, a First World War fighter-pilot who was killed in action. His father, Sir Albert Ball, was an Alderman and was a Mayor, and later Lord Mayor, of Nottingham.

life was affected by personal tragedies, his brother dying young, whilst his son, Captain Albert Ball, was killed in action, aged twenty, in the First World War. He had been one of Britain's outstanding fighter-pilots and was awarded the Victoria Cross.

BAND CONCERTS

The opening of the Arboretum in 1852 was accompanied by concerts from the bands of the Eighth Royal Irish Hussars and the South Notts Yeomanry. The Quadrille Band of Mr Wilson also played on alternate Monday evenings. He was John Mowbray Wilson, 'Professor of Music, Pianoforte and, Brass Instrument Warehouse, Milton Street'.

The gradual increase in the number of public parks was accompanied by regular band concerts, especially in the Castle grounds, and Victoria Embankment. Popular bands included those from local collieries, the City Police and City Transport Departments. The 1930s also saw the establishment of such novelties as piano accordeon bands and carnival bands. These used to hold festivals, with bands competing with each other. Many of these had children as members, and would parade through the streets in marching order.

When the City Council inaugurated Annual Festivals in the 1960s, a number of well-known military bands gave concerts in the Old Market Square.

BANKING

A successful banker has to be able to borrow money at a lower rate of interest than he charges those to whom he lends the money. It is also necessary to ensure that he does not run the risk of being unable to repay the borrowed moneys if required. A Nottingham man, Thomas Smith, was able to fulfil these conditions in such a way that the banking business he started is still operating today. He was born in 1631 in the Nottinghamshire village of Cropwell Butler but his father died when he was still only ten years old. He was then placed in the care of a guardian in Nottingham. When he was old enough he opened a shop in Nottingham, near to what today is Exchange Walk. He was a mercer, which meant he traded mainly in textiles and his shop was close to the market. Thomas became used to having sums of money from his business, which he took care to keep safe. The market traders, who came and went daily, found that Smith would also look after their cash as well and he established a reputation for reliability. He soon recognised as other bankers did, and still do, that all the money deposited with him was not needed to be repaid at the same time. The wider these deposits were collected meant less risk of having to be repaid all at once and Thomas Smith found that he could even give the lenders interest on their money. Most of the money he received from the market traders would be in coin, or even in

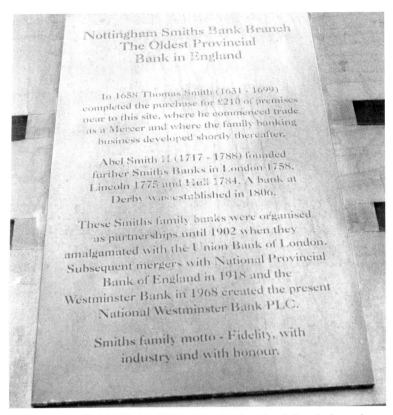

Nottingham Smiths Bank Branch
The Oldest Provincial
Bank in England

In 1658 Thomas Smith (1631 - 1699)
completed the purchase for £210 of premises
near to this site, where he commenced trade
as a Mercer and where the family banking
business developed shortly thereafter.

Abel Smith II (1717 - 1788) founded
further Smiths Banks in London 1758,
Lincoln 1775 and Hull 1784. A bank at
Derby was established in 1806.

These Smiths family banks were organised
as partnerships until 1902 when they
amalgamated with the Union Bank of London.
Subsequent mergers with National Provincial
Bank of England in 1918 and the
Westminster Bank in 1968 created the present
National Westminster Bank PLC.

Smiths family motto - Fidelity, with
industry and with honour.

This plaque is on a wall of the National Westminster Bank on South Parade. It was known as Smith's Bank Branch. Thomas Smith's shop, the first country bank, stood on a nearby site.

precious metals, gold and silver, so he could not of course lend out more than he received. What he could do though was to write out a promise that he would pay in cash the sum mentioned in the note. This note could then be used by the person possessing to use, say for purchase of stocks for his business. This of course was the foundation of banking business, using cheques, bills of exchange (similar to cheques) and bank notes.

The system required confidence that obligations would be met. This Smith and his successors achieved this by careful management. The bank therefore became the first provincial bank in the country, a fact recognised by a plaque on the wall of the Smith's Branch of the National Westminster Bank on South Parade.

Others, in Nottingham and elsewhere, tried to emulate Smith's example, some of whom succeeded and others who did not, with losses being suffered by those who had had lent money.

One bank which was a success was started in Nottingham in the eighteenth century by Ichabod Wright, an ironmonger who like Thomas Smith added banking to his business. The name Ichabod was given to successive descendants, one of whom built Mapperley Hall. The bank was eventually amalgamated with Lloyds Bank.

Hart, Fellows and Company was established in the early nineteenth century. Alfred Thomas Fellows was a sheriff and senior councillor in the pre-1835 corporation and was appointed as the new corporation's treasurer. When he died in 1862 his son John became treasurer, as did his son George in 1874 when his father died. George resigned in 1913 and the City Accountant became the City Treasurer.

A rather different bank was a branch of a national company, Cheque Book Limited. It had two offices, one in Pelham Street and one in Lister Gate. It operated in the same way as the Post Office did with postal orders, by selling cheques of various denominations. Unfortunately, its cheques were too easy to forge and heavy losses caused it to close in 1879.

☞ *See also Farrow's Bank Limited*

BAPTISTS

The freedom of religious worship other than in Anglican churches was established by the Toleration Act of 1689. In Nottingham this led to the founding of two different chapels both known as Independents. Eventually they built their own places of worship on Castle Gate and High Pavement. They still flourish, but with different names and venues.

The eighteenth century, however, saw 'dissent' not only against the churches, but in different ways on theological grounds, leading to several new sects. One of these was the Baptist movement whose believers did not think infant baptism meaningful and preferred adult baptism. Within the movement there were also shades of opinions, leading to the setting up of different groups. One of the earliest, with its chapel on Friar Lane became known as Particular Baptists, as opposed to General or Arminian Baptists. Both groups differed on theological grounds, but did not attract many adherents in the eighteenth century.

The nineteenth century witnessed a religious revival, in both Anglican and Nonconformists, and this, together with an ever increasing population, resulted in much new building of both churches and chapels. The Baptists had built a chapel in 1799 on Park Street (now Friar Lane). This was built by the Particular Baptists, who then moved to larger premises on George Street, with the Scotch Baptists occupying the Park Street premises. The General Baptists built a large building on Plumtree Place off Stoney Street, which later became a school and has recently been refurbished. The Particular Baptists also

This modern Baptist Church at Lenton is in sharp contrast to the style of older churches. Thomas Helwyn, after whom it is named was a member of a family which lived at Broxtowe Hall. He was active in the early seventeenth century in promoting the Baptist movement.

erected a new chapel on Derby Road in 1851. Other Baptist chapels at that time included the Arminian, Broad Street, the Separatists in Paradise Place, and the New Testament Disciples Salem Chapel in Barker Gate.

Other chapels were opened in areas adjoining the borough and when they became part of the borough in 1877, the total number of Baptist chapels was nineteen. The divisions within the movement came to an end in the 1930s after which congregations joined forces.

As with other denominations, the twentieth century with its large-scale demolition of properties in older areas and the transfer of population to new outer areas, saw many Baptist chapels either disappearing or used for other purposes, as well as some new ones being built.

BARLOCK ROAD
In the 1920s a new road was made leading off the right hand side of Arnold Road, Basford. This name reflected the fact that the Barlock Typewriter

Company had built a new factory there. A brochure issued by the company gave details of its 'Byron' model. 'One typewriter does the work of three' proclaimed the advertisement. This referred to three different size length interchangeable carriages. 'Add wings to her hands with the feather touch' it encouragingly added.

In *Wright's Directory* for 1920 under the heading 'typewriter manufacturers' were listed twelve names. This included the Royal Bar-Lock Typewriter Company Limited, 3 Brougham Chambers, Wheeler Gate. It also listed three teachers of typewriting including Miller's Business College. The earliest mention of typewriters in directories is in 1899, under the heading 'TYPE WRITERS'. This gives the names of Johnson and Knight, Misses, Castle Rooms, Lenton Road, presumably two of Nottingham's earliest typists. The earliest mention of typewriters is 1902 when Remington Typewriter Company was listed as at 2 Lister Gate. The Royal Bar-Lock Typewriter Company appears for the first time in a 1907 directory.

Kelly's Directory for 1956, the last one to be published, has five headings for typewriters – agents and dealers, manufacturers, repairs, suppliers and offices. Under 'manufacturers' was 'Byron Business Machines (John Jardine) Limited'. Also included under that heading is a foretaste of the future – IBM United Kingdom Limited (I B M Electric Typewriters) but with only a London address. The directory also included the names of the occupiers of eighty-three houses on Barlock Road.

A directory with a rather different layout than *Kelly's* appeared as a once only issue in July 1967, by Blair Publications. It had one heading – 'Typewriter Manufacturers – Miniature' with a single entry – Petite Typewriters (Byron Business Machines) Limited, Chelsea Street, New Basford. Under 'Typewriters' were named fifteen other companies including I B M United Kingdom Limited – now with an address, Maid Marian Way.

BASFORD

Basford was one of five villages around Nottingham, which became part of the Borough under an Extension Act of 1877. It was a large parish of 2,836 acres, that is, nearly three times as large as the Borough. It was bounded on the south by Lenton, Radford and the Borough. The distance from west to east was two and a quarter miles, stretching from the county border at Broxtowe on the west to the Borough boundary on the east. It was one and a half miles from north to south.

Basford was in the valley of the River Leen, a tributary of the River Trent, which would have been a reason for its earliest settlement being on the river. This would have supplied essential water, would provide fish and eventually played an important part in its economy. It became part of the medieval

Sherwood Forest, not because it was covered with trees, like some parts of the Forest, but to prove its function as part of the royal domain.

The land was not particularly suitable for agriculture, much of it being common land. In 1792 an Enclosure Act, affecting particularly the eastern part of the parish, was followed by the creation of new industrial villages at Carrington and Sherwood. The original settlement near the River Leen had itself become industrialised through the textile trades, mainly because the River Leen could drive mills and supply water for bleaching and dyeing. The beginning of the lace industry in the 1820s resulted in a new village, New Basford, being built about a mile south of the original settlement, which became known, naturally enough, as Old Basford.

The increasing urbanisation of the parish led to the formation of a Local Board of Health in 1856, which started to tackle matters such as highways, cleansing and a cemetery, thus leading to a smoother transition when Basford became part of the Borough. The extension was due partly to the increasing assimilation of manufacture and trade, and partly to the river, which had provided the original site. Ironically, it was man's abuse, which led to it becoming a health hazard from pollution and use as a common sewer.

Basford had also become the headquarters of a Poor Law union of a large number of other parishes. It had been chosen as a suitable place to provide a

Church Street, Basford, seen here thirty years ago, still had reminders of a hundred years earlier.

workhouse for parishes within a radius of about ten miles, as this was felt would be the maximum distance people seeking refuge in the workhouse could be expected to travel. The union became one of the new Boards of Guardians under the Act of 1834, which was to cause an anomaly after Basford became part of Nottingham, which had its own Board of Guardians. Eventually, and not without some resistance, Basford and other parishes were amalgamated with the Nottingham Board. The anomaly still existed to some extent when Basford Rural District Council was formed in 1894, covering the same area as the Guardians. The headquarters of both jointly continued to be in Nottingham.

BATHING

One of the differences in policy of the pre-1835 Corporation and that of the reformed one concerned bathing. In the eighteenth century the Corporation paid Henry Smith and Robert Glover £1.4s for attending the River Trent on twelve Sundays. This was in 1771 and in 1780 constables who had attended at the Trent Bridge and River Leen to prevent people from bathing on Sundays were paid £1.14s.

The new Corporation took a more positive line in May 1844 when a committee reported to the Council that it has looked at several sites for 'cold baths for public bathing'. One such site on the Wells Road was thought to be a very eligible place with a fine spring of pure water with beautiful scenery around it. Another site was the Ozier Holt adjoining the Trent near the *Union Inn*. A plan of 1848 showed this piece of water on the site later to be of Turney's Factory on London Road.

The Council were encouraged to take further steps to provide facilities for bathing by an Act of Parliament, the Baths and Washhouses Act of 1846. The Council adopted this Act in 1849 and new premises were built on Gedling Street. A report in March 1851 stated that the venture was going so well that the demand for the large plunge bath on Saturdays was so great that it was decided to open it, which had not been intended.

The washing department caused some concern in February 1854 because it had no soft water and no working drying apparatus. This led to a recommendation that it be closed. This was not agreed to, after an eloquent speech by the Chairman of the Committee who asked:

What can be more dreary or more unwholesome or more calculated to drive a man away from his own fireside than the accumulated miseries of washing day?

After the Borough Extension of 1877 took place the former parishes wanted baths and Radford Baths on Boden Street was opened in 1880. Bulwell had to be content with a bathing shed on the River Leen at a cost of £50.

Victoria Baths, now re-named Victoria Leisure Centre, was Nottingham's first public baths, erected in 1851 and later re-built in its present form.

The Gedling Street Baths were pulled down in 1894 and a new Victoria Baths built on the site. Other areas of the city had to wait until the twentieth century when new ones were provided at Lenton, Noel Street, the Meadows and Basford. The 1930s saw the opening of open-air lidos at Highfields, Carrington and Bulwell, but only the latter has survived the rigours of the English summer. Washhouses too have disappeared due to laundrettes and domestic washing machines.

BELLFOUNDING

One of Nottingham's skilled trades in medieval times was the casting of bells for churches and other buildings. Nottingham was one of the few towns in England to possess its own bell foundry. A factor which helped to start the industry was the coal to be found around the town.

St Mary's church had a bell earlier than 1394 when Thomas de Downham was alleged to have stolen the bell-clapper. A year earlier Robert de Ayton was summoned for owing two shillings to John Painter for painting a bell of the cross of St Mary's.

Robert Mellers and his brother Richard were both bell-founders in the early sixteenth century. Richard was Mayor in 1506–7 and Robert in 1521–22. When Richard died he left money to his wife, Agnes, to found a Free Grammar School in the town. This later became Nottingham Boys' High School.

The bell-founding business continued in the Mellers family until Elizabeth, daughter of Robert, married Humphrey Quernby who in a deed of 1547 is described as bell-founder. His surname was spelled in several different ways, including 'Querneby' which, as it is the name of a road at Mapperley, seems to be the most appropriate way.

Another family engaged in bell-founding was the Oldfields. George and Henry both appear in documents in the sixteenth and seventeenth centuries. George's foundry was known to be in a yard off Long Row and survived until the end of the eighteenth century.

Although church bells were made in Nottingham for other counties, they were not objects needed frequently, as they lasted for many years. The foundries no doubt made many other similar goods to keep going.

BENDIGO

Will any of today's sporting heroes be remembered 120 years after their deaths by a town named after his pseudonym, by a lion couchant tombstone, by a statue gracing a public house and a portrait painted on a wall? Such is the posthumous fame of William Thompson. Born in Nottingham in 1811 he led a life as varied as his mementos. Much was written about him during his lifetime, some of which was factual. This did not apply to his pseudonym said to have been derived from a forename he did not have. He was alleged to have been one of triplets whose names were the biblical Shadrach, Meshack, and Abednego. The baptism register of St Mary's church reveals the more mundane William and his twin Richard as having been baptised on 16 October 1811, the sons of Benjamin and Mary.

When William was twenty-one he became a prize fighter, a career he followed for sixteen years, becoming All-England champion. He was, however, almost as well known for his court appearances, usually on charges of assault and drunkenness. The reporters of the day usually managed to be present when he appeared and often headed their reports in such terms as 'Bendigo in court again'. The *Nottingham Review* for 1 November 1853 reported 'Bendigo in trouble at Sheffield' and gave an extract from a Sheffield newspaper. On one occasion the reporter quoted him

This memorial to William Thompson was paid for by subscriptions from some of his admirers.

verbatim which shows his command of the Nottingham vernacular. He accused the policeman who arrested him as follows:

Didn't yo' cum to me and tek owd on me at the back o' th' neck and try to throttle me?

Strangely enough, one of Bendigo's favourite occupations was quiet angling in the River Trent where on one occasion he saved a child from drowning. The *Nottingham Journal* was fair to him in 1873 in an article 'Bendigo out of trouble at last'. This referred to an open-air service in Sneinton Market Place when he gave a short sermon 'quite in a style of his own'. He said he had fought for the devil long enough, and now he would fight for Christ. The article commented that he seemed 'sincere, earnest and without hypocrisy'.

When he died in 1880, he was honoured with an obituary in *The Times* and his funeral procession from Beeston to Bath Street cemetery was watched by a crowd of about 20,000 people.

BILBOROUGH

Bilborough was mentioned in Domesday Book when it was, like most villages, quite small. It remained that way and rural for nearly 850 years. It was mainly agricultural land and had close connections with the adjoining village of Strelley. The Edge family of Strelley Hall owned land in most of the two villages.

Both villages had coal deposits fairly close to the surface, which were worked early on by bell-pits, traces of which can sometimes be seen today. When the Nottingham Canal was built in 1794, an arm of the canal was extended into Bilborough where it connected with tramways used for transporting coal. Later a deep coal mine was opened on the edge of the village. This was named Broxtowe Colliery. Broxtowe was the name of the Wapentake in which Bilborough was situated. Wapentakes were meetings, usually held in the open air, where men from the various places met to discuss matters of mutual concern. Broxtowe, though not a village, did have an early existence, which was revealed by excavations to date from British occupation.

Both Bilborough and Broxtowe were to be transformed between 1930 and 1960 by the development of housing estates for Nottingham, as a result of

The old village centre of Bilborough around the church is hidden from the twentieth century housing.

which they became part of the City in 1933. Broxtowe is almost completely residential but Bilborough has, in addition, a part devoted to modern industrial uses.

BIRKIN FAMILY

Richard Birkin, his parents and other relatives came to live in Basford, from their homes in Belper, Derbyshire in the 1820s. They were attracted by the growing machine industry of lace making which was outstripping the declining hosiery trade using stocking frames. He started in a small way in New Basford and later, in partnership with Richard Biddle, built up a large lace manufacturing business. In the 1851 census he was described as employing 88 men, 127 women, 20 boys and 50 girls.

In 1845 he had been elected as an Alderman on the Town Council, one of the few men who were so elected without first having been a Councillor. He was Mayor in 1849, 1855, 1861 and 1862, the only man to occupy that office four times under the reformed council. He purchased property in the growing Lace Market area of Nottingham, and after having Plumtree House demolished, laid out a new thoroughfare called Broadway, connecting Stoney Street and St Mary's Gate. Here he commissioned T C Hine, architect, to design new warehouses on the south side of Broadway. The arch leading into the warehouses has an inscription recording his initials, those of the architect and of the builder.

Richard also became a director of the Midland Railway. By 1861 he had retired and was living at Aspley Hall, a mansion on Lord Middleton's estate. He died on 8 October 1870 and was buried in the General Cemetery on the same day as his second wife, Eliza, who died two days after her husband. Richard was aged sixty-four and his wife sixty.

Richard's son, Thomas Isaac, was born at Basford in 1832 and carried on the family business. After his father's death he greatly expanded the lace business, including setting up subsidiaries abroad. He was also actively engaged in public duties. He was chairman of Nottingham School of Art, High Sheriff in 1892 and a Deputy Lieutenant. He was an early Commandant of the Robin Hood Rifle Corps. He supported charities including the General Hospital and the Children's Hospital, to which he gave Forest House, off Mapperley Road. He was made a Baronet, the Baronetcy of which still survives. Some of his children and grandchildren have had notable careers in the two World Wars.

He lived for a number of years at Ruddington Grange and died in 1922, leaving an estate of over £2 million pounds.

The archway leading to the former lace warehouses on Broadway has reminders of the Birkin family. R B is the father Richard and T B his son Thomas (later Sir Thomas Isaac Birkin). The initials of the architect and builder are also there.

BOOT, JESSE

Born in 1850, Jesse was the son of a father who died when Jesse was only thirteen years old. With his mother they ran a herbalist's shop in Goose Gate. He soon showed signs that he was determined to become a successful businessman. He developed the herbalist's business by innovative methods such as pre-packing Epsom salts, reducing prices and extensive advertising. After legislation allowed him to employ a qualified pharmacist, he was able to expand the chemist's side of the business.

In 1892 he started to expand his retail empire and by 1897 had nine shops in Nottingham and others throughout Britain. He also started manufacturing pharmaceuticals, at first in part of a former factory on Station Street but later on a nearby site on Island Street, in purpose-built premises. (These were demolished a few years ago for a large new development, called The Island.

This already has BBC East Midlands TV and Radio, a hotel, offices of the East Midlands Development Association, and a walk-in Health Centre, with more to come.)

In the early years of the twentieth century, Boots, emblazoned in the familiar copperplate script, was the largest pharmaceutical chain in the world. By 1931 it had a thousand branches. It was well managed, with carefully chosen heads of department, which ensured large profits. Jesse was to use his share to a great extent on charitable ventures, for which he received a knighthood, a baronetcy and in 1929 a peerage. This followed perhaps his most outstanding benefaction, the building of new premises for the University College of Nottingham at Highfields in Lenton. He died in 1931, after years of crippling illness.

He was succeeded by his son, the second Lord Trent, as chairman of the company. Its premises in Nottingham eventually occupied most of Station Street, but have now become part of Capital One. Boots' new premises were erected in the 1930s onwards, partly in the City and partly in Beeston. These include buildings listed for their innovative designs.

And the Doctor said

"Get it carefully prepared" at Boots, Pelham St.

Where prescriptions are made up by chemists qualified by Pharmaceutical Society's examination. The charge is about one half the usual chemist's charges — but BOOTS, CASH CHEMISTS, wish you to note the excellence of the method of dispensing more than the cost.

PURE DRUGS, PATENT MEDICINES, TOILET REQUISITES, SURGICAL APPLIANCES, CHOICE PERFUMES, &c., at great reductions from ordinary chemist's prices.

SPEAKING OF PRESCRIPTIONS.

You hold a prescription from a doctor in whom you have full confidence, and you feel sure you will be all right again soon.

But you want relief quickly, and that prescription requires preparing promptly. In any case you want it carefully dispensed, and you do not want to pay more than the ingredients and the service are worth.

Boots CASH CHEMISTS,

2-10 Pelham Street; 16 Albert Street; 69 Long Row; 16-20 Goose Gate; 1 Arkwright Street; 159 Alfreton Road; 88 St. Ann's Well Road; 253 Mansfield Road; 7 London Road, **NOTTINGHAM.**

BOOTS Ltd., Proprietors, Head Offices, Nottingham.   JESSE BOOT, Managing Director.

This advertisement, dated 1903, shows how far Jesse Boot's empire had then grown from the small herbal shop.

BOOTH, WILLIAM

William Booth was born in 1829 at Nottingham. At the age of thirteen he was apprenticed to a pawnbroker. He attended the Wesleyan Chapel in Broad Street where a revivalist meeting influenced him to devote his life to helping those who needed help either because of poverty, homelessness, drunkenness or any of the wretched ways of life which the mid-nineteenth century offered. When his apprenticeship ended he went to London to work and his connection with Nottingham was severed until 1905 when, as General William Booth, he returned to be granted the freedom of the City.

His title of General was part of the driving force of the Salvation Army, which he formed as a wager of war against the many social evils he wished to tackle, combined with a Christian belief. He had married in 1855 and with his wife, Catherine, they travelled abroad on preaching missions. On their return to England, Booth recognised that there was a need for his mission in England, just as much as abroad. He published an indictment against the conditions, especially in the East End of London, entitling his book *In Darkest England and The Way Out*. He started the periodical *The War Cry* and set-up the organisation known as the Salvation Army. Despite military sounding titles, their adherents were only like the traditional army in their purposefulness in carrying out work without flinching.

The statue of the founder of the Salvation Army, William Booth, stands in front of his birthplace in Notintone Place.

William and Catherine Booth had eight children and they all became active in the movement. Catherine died in 1890 and William in 1912 at the age of eighty-three.

BOULEVARDS

The Bill to extend the Borough boundaries of Nottingham was deposited in Parliament in December 1876. The following February the Extension Committee which had negotiated the proceedings reported to the Council that they had had discussions with the Trustees of the Gregory Estate. The

Borough's northern boundary was on the edge of the Racecourse and Recreation Ground, now known as The Forest, whilst Gregory's Trustees owned the adjoining land. The Council had proposed making a new sixty feet wide road to connect Mansfield Road and Alfreton Road. This would take in some land belonging to the Trustees and it was agreed that an exchange of a small portion of Corporation land with the Trustees would be of mutual advantage. Thus was born Gregory Boulevard.

At the same time, the Council had agreed with the Lenton Local Board that a similar arrangement should take place, to enable a new road to connect the Borough with Lenton, alongside the Nottingham Canal. This was desirable because it was a flat site, whilst the existing route was along the steep Derby Road, an important factor in the days of horse-drawn traffic. This was done and became the new road named Lenton Boulevard. No doubt the work of Baron Haussman, who had created a system of boulevards in Paris, influenced the Council to link the two boulevards with two more to form three sides of a square which would avoid through traffic having to negotiate Nottingham's still medieval street pattern. The two new boulevards were named Lenton and Radford, and the earlier Lenton Boulevard was renamed Castle Boulevard.

This early example of enlightened town planning was to be complemented fifty years later by a similar, but outer, ring system, consisting of Clifton Boulevard, Middleton Boulevard, Western Boulevard and Valley Road. This was finally completed in the 1960s when the Clifton Bridge over the River Trent enabled the A52 road to be joined up, including Nottingham's first flyover, with Clifton Boulevard.

BOUNDARIES – MAPS

Speed's map of 1610 shows the medieval street pattern but only shows the built-up area of the borough. The common lands which extended as far as Nottingham Forest in the north and the River Trent to the south, were excluded.

Tarbotton's map of 1876, drawn up for the Borough's extension Parliamentary Bill, is the first map to show details of the whole of the borough boundary as well as those of the adjoining villages brought within the boundary of the borough.

Ordnance Survey maps from 1881 onwards show two subsequent additions to the City boundary, as extended in 1932 and 1952.

BREWHOUSE YARD

When the Normans built Nottingham Castle, it and some of the adjoining land did not, as a royal property, become subject to the jurisdiction of the borough. It eventually ceased to be of use to the monarchy and it passed into private hands. This included a small area at the foot of the Castle rock on which stood the Castle's brewery. As it was outside the borough, when an outbreak of plague occurred in 1610, Brewhouse Yard did not receive any financial help as did people in the borough, from a special relief fund. However, the County Magistrates contributed £22.10s 8d 'towards the ayde and releife of the people under the Castle'.

In 1617 the borough made some approaches to try and purchase Brewhouse Yard but these were unsuccessful. Although as what was known as an extra parochial place, the inhabitants of the few houses did not have to pay rates, this was not an unmixed blessing. It became a notorious place from the activities of those seeking a refuge from law and order.

In *Wright's Directory* for 1832, it was described as having eighty inhabitants, several dye-houses and two public houses, one of which was the *Trip to Jerusalem* and the other the *Gate*. One of these was said to have a room

The area at the foot of the castle rock was an extra parochial district until it was brought into the borough. The eighteenth century houses, after serving the Corporation Water Department, have been converted into a Museum of Nottingham Life.

cut in the rock with a hole at the top to admit light and so called the *Star Parlour*. It also quoted from *Dr Thoroton's Antiquties* that Brewhouse Yard had once been an asylum for a fraternity of fanatics called Philadelphians or the Family of Love. They professed that their love was

to all men, be they ever so wicked and that they obeyed all magistrates, even tyrannical ones, without regard to whether they were Jews, Gentiles or Turks.

They seem to have been a few hundred years too soon.

Brewhouse Yard was on the bank of the River Leen and the Old Waterworks Company had recently built a new engine house. Along with other extra parochial places, it lost that appellation by Act of Parliament in 1868. The Waterworks Company was later taken over by Nottingham Corporation Water Department as its offices. When water supply was taken over, in 1974, by Severn Trent Water Authority, the offices and the adjoining eighteenth century cottages were handed over to the Arts and Museums Department of the City Council. The cottages have been transformed into a museum depicting social life throughout the ages, with different rooms showing various earlier uses. A house at the west end of the attractively laid out grounds is a replica of a nineteenth century schoolroom.

BREWING

The earliest written evidence of the activities of brewers is in a record of 8 October 1395 of presentments to the Mayor at a Great Tourn by the Mickleton Jury. The Great Tourn was a meeting at which complaints were made to the Mayor by a body known as the Mickleton Jury. They acted in much the same way as today consumer's associations and trades inspectors do. In this instance, the Jury said on oath that all the brewers were guilty because 'they brew against the assize and sold with cups and dishes'. The assize of ale was a regulation covering the method of brewing, and the price of beer and how it was sold. The selling of it in cups and dishes was prohibited because they could not be sealed.

What penalty was imposed on the brewers was not stated, but the practice continued as similar presentments were made later. Another complaint, in January 1020, was that 'Nicholas Draper had been brewing in a little house without a chimney, to the great danger of his neighbours' for which he was fined three shillings and four pennies.

The earliest record of a brewery being built as such was one known as Green's Brewery in Butcher's Close. This was near the junction today of Lower Parliament Street and London Road. It was built to a design by William Stretton in 1795.

The earliest mention of brewers in street directories is in *White's* volume for 1832, where under the heading 'brewers', it states 'see Porter Dealers', where there are only five names, one of which was Deverill and Company, Brewers of ale and Porter, Pelham Street. *Orange's Directory* of 1840 lists eight breweries, none of which survived to be mentioned in 1852. In that year, a new brewery was started in New Basford, which was to celebrate its centenary with a booklet recording its history. This was Shipstone's Brewery, a name which was to become almost synonymous with Nottingham ale, universally known as 'Shippo's'. James Shipstone, the founder, with his son, also James, and another son, Thomas, were able to form a Joint Stock Company in 1880. A well-known feature of Shipstone's Brewery was its drays drawn by Shire horses. The Brewery suffered a severe loss in 1914 when the horses were called up for war service, many of them never to return.

One of the well-known Nottingham nineteenth century breweries was that of Shipstones, with its landmark tower.

The company took over Carrington Brewery and later, in the 1920s, Beeston Brewery and George Hooley's.

A grandson of the founder, Thomas, took over as Chairman in 1922. He became active in public affairs in Nottingham and was made a knight. His daughter, Mrs A E Snell, has written a book, *The Velvet Years*, which gives details of the family's life in the early twentieth century.

Shipstone's Brewery on Radford Road, with its tall tower, was a monumental sight, with its sign 'Star Brewery'. The tower is still there, but some of the associated buildings have been demolished and replaced by new houses. This followed the take over of the business in the 1990s by Greenall Whitley when brewing was discontinued. Part of the premises are now used as auction rooms.

In the first *Wright's directory* after the borough boundary was extended in 1877, there were nineteen firms listed under the heading 'brewers'. Most of these, however, were Nottingham offices or agents of breweries at Burton-on-Trent, Kimberley and Newark. Only one of the actual Nottingham breweries survived into the second half of the twentieth century. This was the Nottingham Brewery, later taken over by Whitbreads. The premises on Mansfield Road were demolished in the 1960s and York House erected on the site.

Another brewery, which had a number of public houses in the City, was the Home Brewery. Their premises were, however, just outside the City boundary at Daybrook, but the brewery had maltings at Old Basford. The Daybrook building, a large modern one, is now occupied by offices of Nottinghamshire County Council, following the takeover of the Home Brewery. The Basford maltings building has been converted into dwellings for students.

More recently brewing has returned to Nottingham to cater for real ale drinkers in a microbrewery, Castle Rock, on Queens Bridge Road, with its own brands of beer.

BROAD MARSH

The name dates back to as early as the fourteenth century, from the Latin *Magnus Marescus* but translated in early English to Broddemarshe. It was the southern end of the Saxon borough and its marshiness was due to its nearness to the River Leen and the sandstone cliff above it of Low and Middle Pavements. The rain would percolate the sandstone just as water would the drainage of the town. This would not have made it a desirable place to live in, as witnessed by the slum dwellings of the nineteenth century. The nearby Plum, Pear, Peach and Currant Street were not as rural as they sounded.

Most of the small, overcrowded and insanitary houses were demolished in the 1930s and the cleared site became a 'temporary' bus station. The creation of the Broad Marsh Shopping Mall in the 1960s cleared the remaining properties in the area. All that remains of Broad Marsh is a section off Lister Gate for a few yards with its original nameplate.

Planning permission has recently been given for a comprehensive redevelopment of the shopping mall.

Broad Marsh: there is only a short stretch of a few yards of the original thoroughfare off Lister Gate.

BROMLEY HOUSE

On Angel Row, one hundred yards from the Old Market Square is one of Nottingham's finest buildings. Bromley House is a listed building, grade II* which indicates it is of special interest. It was built in 1752 for Sir George Smith, baronet, the grandson of the founder of Smith's Bank, a later building of which still stands on South Parade as Smith's Branch of the National Westminster Bank. Sir George's son, also named George, inherited money from a member of the Bromley family. He changed his surname and re-named the Angel Row house Bromley House.

The house in red brick originally had railings at the front with steps down to the basement rooms. These have long since disappeared as have the ground floor windows, the rooms of which have been used as shops. It is five storeys high with five bays on the first floor with triangular pediments, five plain bays on the second floor and above the parapet three dormer windows.

The elegant front door with a fanlight opens to a hall, which runs through to a rear door and leads to a long garden. The main staircase leads off to the right from the hall, with other staircases higher up.

Bromley House was used as a town house until, after a period of non-occupation, it was sold in 1820, when it was bought by Nottingham Subscription Library and used by them ever since. Over the years it has also been used for other purposes and these have been described in *Bromley House 1752–1991* edited by Rosaly T Coope and Jane Y Corbett.

The garden of Bromley House is only a few yards away from the busy Angel Row.

Since the book was published, one of the upper rooms, formerly used by The Thoroton Society of Nottinghamshire, has been re-furbished and named The Thoroton Room.

☛ *See also Libraries; Mechanics' Institute; Photography*

BULWELL

Bulwell, like Basford, was a Leen Village, which had been settled in Anglo-Saxon times. It, too, benefited from the water of the River Leen and was to become a part of Nottingham in 1877. It differed in some ways because it also had extractive industries in coal, quarrying for building stone and lime burning. It also differed in not having a common boundary with the Borough. This, and its distance from the centre of the borough no doubt caused something of the antipathy of its Local Board to the proposal to bring Bulwell into the borough. It decided to make official opposition to the Parliamentary Bill for extension. However, the Borough Council let it be known that if Bulwell did not want to be part of the Borough, so be it. The Bulwell Board no doubt reflected on this and eventually decided not to proceed with opposition, in the expectation that Bulwell might benefit from the extension.

This small house near the Market Place has walls of Bulwell stone and brick and a pantiled roof.

BURGESSES

Domesday Book records that in the reign of Edward the Confessor, that is before the Normans invaded England, Nottingham had 173 burgesses and nineteen villages. Although literally 'burgess' meant an inhabitant of a borough, the term in Nottingham referred to a special status of some of the inhabitants. They had full municipal rights, which the villagers or villeins had not. The latter had to perform certain duties and were not free men, as the burgesses were.

When Nottingham received various privileges from royal Charters, these were addressed to the burgesses who eventually became the equivalent of the local council, subject later to the jurisdiction of the mayor and aldermen. They were the only inhabitants who could vote at Parliamentary elections until 1835. The method of becoming a burgess in the earliest years is not certain but eventually the rules were that a man must be of full age, twenty-one, or the eldest son of a burgess or had served an apprenticeship. The Council or Common Hall as it became known did however elect others as burgesses, either as a special honour or on payment of a sum of money. Some of the burgesses also had the privilege of using a part of the common lands as meadow for grazing or other agricultural use. These were known as burgess parts. The whole system of town government was reformed in 1835, with more democratic elections and the term 'burgess' was replaced by 'freeman'.

☛ *See also Enclosure*

BURIAL GROUNDS

Until the end of the medieval period, the dead were buried beneath the floor of the parish church. With increased population this became impractical and graveyards adjoining the church established. Nottingham had only three Anglican churches, St Mary, St Peter and St Nicholas, each with its own graveyard. The considerable increase in the population from the mid-eighteenth century onwards resulted in the graveyards becoming full, especially in the most populated parish, St Mary. Accordingly, other plots of land were brought into service as additional burial grounds, as they became known, rather than as graveyards.

These too soon became full and later in the nineteenth century they had to be closed to further burials. Two of these were on Barker Gate, one of which has been landscaped with seats, whilst the other one has been grassed, at the corner of Barker Gate and Bellar Gate as a street improvement and provides a colour display of crocus in Spring. One at the bottom of Barker Gate formed part of the site of the 1930s Ice Stadium and the part immediately in front of the Stadium remained as a disused burial ground until the 1960s when the remains of the interred were removed and the site became a car park.

The former burial ground on Barker Gate has been grassed and is a blaze of colour in Spring with crocuses.

In 1832, following an outbreak of cholera in the town more room was needed for burials. Samuel Fox, a member of the Society of Friends, owned a field at the bottom of St Ann's Well Road, which he gave to St Mary's Church for a burial ground. When it was completed it was consecrated as an Anglican burial ground and Samuel Fox found that this excluded non-conformist clergymen from conducting funeral services. With other men, he was instrumental in forming a public company to provide the General Cemetery at Canning Circus.
☛ *See also Cemeteries*

BYRON, GEORGE GORDON NOEL, 6TH BARON
Born in 1788, Byron the poet lived as a boy for a short time in Nottingham, a Holbrook bequest plaque outside the house where he stayed commemorating this. He had a rather unhappy childhood and it may be that this influenced the poem which he wrote there:

In Nottingham town, quite close to Swine Green,
Lives as cursed an old woman as ever was seen
When she dies which I hope will be quite soon,
She fondly believes she will fly to the moon.

Swine Green was a small area at the top of what are now Victoria Street and Pelham Street.

CABS

The restricted area of the borough until the middle of the nineteenth century meant that most of the inhabitants lived and worked within such a confined area that they seldom needed transport. The better-off, of course, could afford to keep horses, either for riding to travel further afield or pulling conveyances such as carriages. Those who did not possess such luxuries could, in times of necessity, hire a horse-drawn vehicle from what were known as livery stables.

The growing population and trade by 1832 was recognised in *White's Directory* of that year when it recorded:

hackney carriages were first established in the town on New Year's Day 1825 by Mr John King. They are here called 'Flys' and are tolerably well employed owing to many of the merchants and manufacturers being now resident in the skirts of the town and in the neighbouring parishes.

It listed three such stands, at the *Lion Hotel*, at the *George IV* in Castle Gate and in the Market Place. They were called hackney carriages, hackney being used to mean horses, as hacking was used to mean riding. These were the forerunners of today's taxis.

Such amenities were more usually called 'cabs' an abbreviation of 'cabriolet'. In 1852 a committee of the Town Council recommended that the cabriolets and other carriages plying for hire be registered, licensed and numbered, and that the drivers wear a badge, their numbers being limited to forty. The Committee had been appointed in response to a request from the manager of the Midland Railway that cab proprietors and drivers be controlled and kept on stands, to prevent annoyances to passengers.

The Council no doubt expected the cab proprietors to provide stands with shelters for the cab drivers. However, as late as 1877 it was recorded that a cabmen's shelter was to be erected on Station Street with a gift of £75 from William Pyatt and £81 13s collected by Mrs Morse for the same purpose. She was the wife of the Reverend Francis Morse, Vicar of St Mary's. She, with other ladies in the town, took an active interest in social work for the welfare of the poor.

☛ *See also Town and County Social Guild*

CAFÉS

The *Oxford English Dictionary* gives 1816 as the date when the word café entered the English language, as a translation of the French coffee house. It was to be many years before Nottingham's inhabitants ceased to regard anything labelled as of French origin without suspicion of immorality. The habit of eating out did start to become fashionable later in the nineteenth century but in establishments known as eating houses. *Wright's Directory* of 1864 lists nineteen of them under the heading 'Eating and Coffee Houses'.

By 1881 the list of 'Eating and Dining Rooms' had grown to forty-three, including some in the extended parts of the Borough such as Radford and Basford. The Nottingham Café Company premises on Long Row were one of five establishments of the company, including the Tram Restaurant, St Peters Square, the Dining Hall, Byard Lane and the Livingstone Coffee Tavern on St Ann's Well Road. There were also two temperance taverns, although presumably all of the others did not have licences for alcoholic drinks. A continental touch was added with the Café Luxemburg on Derby Road.

The Byard Lane Dining Hall had been the source of controversy when it was founded as the owner unilaterally altered the name of Byard Lane to Dining Hall Street, which the Town Council promptly ordered its deletion on the grounds that the owner was seeking free advertising.

The 1920s and 1930s saw a substantial increase in the number of cafés in the City, although the *Kelly's Directory* 1936 listed them under the leading 'Restaurants, Refreshment Rooms, Cafés etc.' There were sixty-two in the list, including a dozen in and around the Old Market Square. These included the Mikado, the Oriental, Kardomah, Savoy and Windmill. The only one in the list of those around the City Centre, which has survived until today, was Griffin and Spalding's on Long Row, now Debenham's.

When the Oriental Café was demolished its very fine ceiling was saved and re-erected elsewhere. Many of the Cafés in the 1936 list survived until at least 1956, when an updated list numbered 128. This reflected the increased popularity of eating out which arose, in many cases, during the Second World War, from food shortages and rationing.

This trend has grown considerably since then as can be seen from the 2003–4 telephone directory which now has a classified section. There are fifty cafés in the City, whilst restaurants are classified into Fast Food (four), General (over one hundred) as well as takeaways and those, which will deliver to you. The cosmopolitan character of Nottingham today is reflected in the number of specialised restaurants offering food from all over the world. To all these must be added the number of public houses which offer meals, compared with fifty or sixty years ago, when food in a public house was usually a packet of crisps or a cheese cob.

CANALS

On 6 May 1788 the Corporation appointed a committee to consider making a canal from the River Trent to the town. On 25 July the committee did not think it proper to engage in an affair of such magnitude as principals but the Hall said it would be willing to lend their assistance to any plan that would appear to them to be of public utility.

Two years later, concerned that coal which came to Nottingham from Derbyshire via the Erewash Canal would jeopardise Nottinghamshire collieries, the Hall called a public meeting on 16 October 1790 to consider a scheme for making a canal from the Cromford Canal direct to Nottingham. It was also asked to approve making a branch canal from Beeston to the proposed Nottingham one. This would remove the difficulty of boats from Nottingham to Beeston due to the awkward nature of Trent Bridge with its many small arches.

As a result an Act of Parliament was obtained in May 1792, although the promoters of the company had to omit the Beeston Canal because of opposition from other established companies. The latter was authorised by another Act in 1794. The Nottingham Canal had an authorised capital of £50,000 and Nottingham Corporation bought some shares in the company, although it was so short of money it had to borrow to do so.

The famed canal engineer, William Jessop, was appointed to carry out the scheme and the first section, from the River Trent to the wharves in Nottingham. It finally cost £80,000 and although the company at one time informed William Jessop that it was much dissatisfied with the erroneous construction of many works, both the Nottingham and Beeston Canals were open by April 1796. The Nottingham Canal was fourteen and three-quarter miles long from Nottingham to Langley Mill and entered Nottinghamshire at Wollaton.

A number of small branches were cut in Nottingham itself, one called Poplar and another, Brewery, went northwards from London Road, where the main branch went southwards to the River Trent. They later became part of the small industrial suburb around what became Poplar Street and Island Street.

The canal prospered for a time but like most canals suffered from competition from the railways from 1841. The company was bought out by Ambergate and Manchester Railway, which abandoned the canal in 1937. After the Second World War, canals were nationalised and the British Waterways Board now own the Nottingham and Beeston Canals. The Nottingham arm from Lenton northwards, where it joined the Beeston cut, was mainly filled in apart from a few stretches further north.

The recent re-building on both sides of the Nottingham Canal between London Road and Lenton have resulted in a revival of the canal for fishing

The view of Nottingham Canal from Wilford Street shows one of the locks and old and new buildings on the north bank.

and pleasure boats, and the parts on the eastern side of London Road near the former railway stations have been altered as part of the Island development on the former Boots factories and warehouses.

The towpath now provides a pleasant walk from London Road to the Beeston Canal.

CASTLE, NOTTINGHAM

The definitive history of the Castle built by the Normans has been published jointly by the Thoroton Society of Nottinghamshire and Nottingham Civic Society. The first edition appeared as Volume 93 of the Thoroton Society's *Transactions* for 1989 and in 1999 a second edition with additional material was issued as a separate book. Both editions were written by Christopher Drage and the additional material by Trevor Foulds.

When the Normans came to Nottingham in 1067 they found that the Anglo-Saxons already had a borough on a commanding site overlooking the

Trent Valley and on a sheer sandstone cliff which made defence easy. The Normans did not seek to extend the borough but instead built a castle on a similar defensible rock, half a mile west of what became known as the English Borough. The area to the east of the Castle was laid out with streets and became the French Borough. Centuries later the two became united, although with some differences retained.

William the Conqueror built castles as part of his campaign to subdue the English Lords. The one at Nottingham was part of this but it was also a permanent residence for kings, when on tours through the country and an administrative headquarters. It was started as a relatively simple large mound, called a motte, and two baileys on which later buildings were erected. As a royal castle, detailed records of the time and the cost of the building as a permanent structure have survived. The Castle was handed over to William

Nottingham Castle, built by the Normans, was demolished after the Civil War, but excavations in 1976 revealed some of the foundations. These were covered up again but their position is shown on the Green by lines of stones.

Peveril as constable and monarchs down to the reign of Henry VIII visited it from time to time. Many stirring events took place at the Castle during the often-troubled centuries of medieval England. In later centuries the kings had other royal residences, and the need for a fortress castle lessened. By 1525 Nottingham Castle was described as in 'decay and ruin'.

The Castle was sold to the Earl of Rutland and then played an important part in the Civil Wars as a stronghold for the Parliamentary forces under Colonel Hutchinson. After the war, the Castle was demolished and following the Restoration of the Monarchy, after the Commonwealth period, the site was given to the Duke of Newcastle.

CASTLE, THE NEW

When the first Civil War ended in 1646, the Castle was kept on as a garrison, although it was not in a good state of repair. However, after being repaired in 1648 it remained in good order until 1651, when it was demolished.

After the restoration of the monarchy in 1662, the ruins of the old Castle and its grounds were the property of the Duke of Buckingham. He sold them to William Cavendish, Earl of Newcastle. Because of his support of royalty he was created the first Duke of Newcastle in 1665. In 1674 he cleared the site and commenced building a ducal mansion, which he insisted was to be called Nottingham Castle, and which was not completed until after his death in 1679. It is believed to have been designed by a Lincoln mason, Samuel Marsh. Although the building showed European influences the Duke himself must have had a large say in the design as, when he died, he left instructions in his Will that it was to be completed according to plans which had been drawn up.

Successive Dukes of Newcastle resided in the Castle during the eighteenth century for a time. The Castle was important to the town not only for itself, but because it influenced others to build fashionable dwellings nearby, at a time when Nottingham was starting to become an attractive town to live in. A good example is Newdigate House on Castle Gate, built for a family of that name who had a mansion at Arbury in Warwickshire. Some of the architectural features, such as pediments, are similar in style to some of the Castle.

The Dukes of Newcastle had other mansions, in central Nottinghamshire and elsewhere and they also preferred the social life of London. The last great social occasion at the Castle was a Ball in 1776 and after that the families no longer resided there. The Castle was let out as apartments and a number of smaller buildings were erected in the grounds. In 1832 the fourth Duke of Newcastle, a right wing Tory, incurred the wrath of a Nottingham mob when he voted against the Bill in Parliament to reform the House of Commons. They stormed the Castle, burned it and it remained a roofless ruin until 1876. After a successful Art Exhibition in 1872, steps were taken

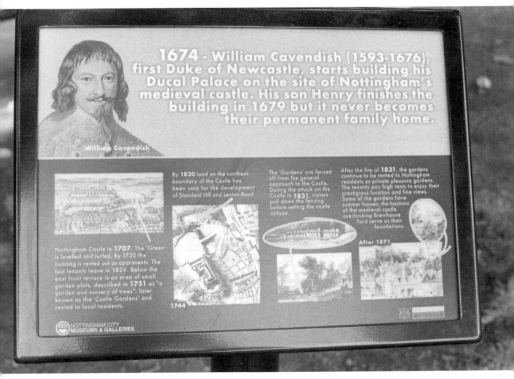

An information board in the Castle grounds describes the history of the building of the mansion by the Duke of Newcastle.

to acquire a suitable building for a permanent art gallery. An agreement was reached in 1875 for the Corporation to acquire the Castle and its grounds on a 500-year lease for 'purposes connected with the advancement of literature, science and art'. The Corporation had to restore the Castle, the work being entrusted to Thomas Chambers Hine, who had worked for the Duke of Newcastle to develop the land to the west of the Castle as the Park Estate. In June 1878, the restored building was declared open as the Castle Museum by the Prince and Princess of Wales, (later King Edward VII and Queen Alexandra). In honour of the occasion the Mayor, James Oldknow, was granted a knighthood.

Since then the grounds have been landscaped, paths made, trees planted and a bandstand erected. Numerous special exhibitions of objects of art and paintings have been held. Examples of work by local artists have been collected and re-furbishments of the rooms have been made. The Castle, with its extensive views of the countryside to the south and west, and the attractive grounds have made it a popular attraction, only a few hundred yards from the city centre.

In 1976 a large excavation of the grounds to the north of the Castle took place and revealed traces of the medieval Castle. Although these had to be filled in, steps have been taken to show something of the layout of the 'place full royal'.

CATERING COMMITTEE

On the 25 January 1915 Councillor R H Swain addressed a meeting of twenty-nine men, consisting of aldermen, councillors, army officers and businessmen. He said he had been appointed by the Local Emergency Committee to form a Catering Committee for feeding families from Lincolnshire in the event of impending or actual invasion of the shores of this country by the Germans.

He had sent a circular to schools, halls and other public buildings, which could be made available for this purpose. It was decided that the town should be divided into three divisions, corresponding to the Parliamentary constituencies. The influence of the military men seems to be reflected in the divisional structure, which was set-up. Each division was to have a Divisional Superintendent, there was to be a Chief Supervisor, Quartermaster in Chief, with a Purchase Committee to find out the amount of food desirable for adults and children (couldn't they have asked their wives?).

The Committee met again twice in February when it was decided to ask the Lincolnshire police to tell evacuees to bring a knife, fork, spoon and drinking vessel.

The Committee did not meet again until March 1916, with three meetings at one of which the form of specimen food tickets and identity cards were shown and illustrated in the minutes. There were no further meetings, not even to record the Committee's demise.

CATTLE MARKET

As the county town and the only borough in the south of the county, Nottingham from earliest times had been the trading centre, and a market town. King Henry II in his Charter of c.1160 stipulated that the men of Nottinghamshire and Derbyshire ought to come to the Borough on Friday and Saturday with their wains (carts) and packhorses.

When the English and French boroughs were united the large open space in the centre became the market place, one of the largest in the country. Dr Charles Deering in his *History of Nottingham*, published in 1751, gave a graphic description of the layout and activities, which took place on market days. Apart from food from farms and manufactured goods, animals of all kinds were bought and sold. Different parts of the market were set aside for the kinds of animals, 'horses, sheep, pigs and cattle'. West of the Horse-Market on Fryer-Row and Angel Row was the Beast Market. Badder and Peat's plan of 1744 clearly shows the position of Fryer-Row, as it was more usually spelled, and it was more frequently referred to as Beastmarket Hill, a name still in use.

In 1835 the Corporation had already started to purchase land on Burton Leys with a view to forming a cattle market there. However, this had to wait until the area of Burton Leys had been made available for building under the Enclosure Act of 1845. A new street was laid out called Burton Street and the cattle market was established there by 1855. It remained there until 1885 when the site was used for the erection of a new Guildhall, which is still the administrative headquarters of Nottingham City Council.

A new cattle market was therefore built on a site at Eastcroft, extending to Meadow Lane. Marriott Ogle Tarbolton, the Borough Surveyor had recommended the site and urged that an abattoir be included. It was, but only fifty years later.

The cattle market is still there and is a hive of activity on Saturday mornings with auctions and stalls selling various goods – but not cattle.
☛ *See also Abattoir*

CAVES
Nottingham has for centuries been known as a place containing caves. Much has been written about them, some of the accounts being factual. One early reference, which was not, was by a Welsh monk, Asser. He claimed that there had been a settlement long before the recorded Anglo-Saxon one and that because the people inhabited them, it was given a British name Tigguacobauce. This merely meant 'a place of caves' and was not an earlier name for Snotingeham (as the Normans spelled Nottingham).

The caves, although a more accurate name for many of them is 'cellars', are all man-made and although some are perhaps a thousand years old, most of them were made between 1600 and 1900. They were formed because the old centre of the borough was built on sandstone, which could fairly easily be dug out as sand, the space caused by this proving useful for storage. They were usually made by horizontal excavations into cliff faces.

Many excavations have been made revealing such caves or cellars, often during redevelopment of sites. *Sandstone Caves of Nottingham* by Tony Waltham, published in 1992, contains plans and photographs of a number of sites, which became available for inspection in this way.

This includes a plan of a former sand mine starting on Peel Street and extending southwards for about 270 metres, in a south-easterly direction. Access to the cellar at the lower end had been made from the basements of

This nineteenth century engraving shows some of the caves known as the Rock Holes in the Park.

shops on Mansfield Road. This complex was used during the Second World War as an air-raid shelter.

There is no trace of any connections between caves for any great distance, despite the lurid accounts from time to time of men going into a cellar and going from one to another, only to emerge miles away from where they started, their hair having been turned white by the experience.

When demolitions of property took place to enable the Broad Marsh Shopping Centre to be built, a number of caves were discovered which entailed a great deal of work to remove tons of debris. These caves have now been put to good use by being opened up for public access.

CEMETERIES

Although one dictionary defines 'cemetery' as 'any burial ground', this section refers to those in Nottingham, which are called by that name, burial grounds being dealt with under that heading. In that section the building of a burial ground on Bath Street as an additional one for St Mary's parish is described as having been made possible by Samuel Fox giving a piece of land for that. He was a Quaker and when he found that consecration had taken place by an Anglican Bishop, he realised that it could not be used by members of his society.

He, along with others, took steps to have built a cemetery to which such restrictions did not apply. In 1836, thirty-seven of the leading men of the town, aldermen, bankers and ministers of various denominations, applied to Parliament to form a proprietary company. The Act was obtained and a company with 440 shares of £10 each was formed. The company purchased land at the summit of Derby Road, which sloped down eastwards to Waverley Street. Part of the land was subject to common rights and the company paid £251 to the Corporation to extinguish the rights.

The Church Cemetery has some striking examples of the monumental mason's art.

The first burial took place in 1838, part of the cemetery being consecrated by the Archbishop, another part being available for funeral services to be conducted by ministers of any religion. In 1840 the company asked the Corporation to release common rights on more land to provide for separate graves for poor families:

> *The interest which the poorer classes take in having separate graves is proved by the way which those in the cemetery have been adorned with flowers, plants or other tokens of affection.*

The site of twelve acres was laid out with winding paths, two mortuary chapels and a lodge. By 1923 about 150,000 people had been buried in the cemetery including a number of notable men and women whose tombstones still remain in situ. Others have been placed alongside the southern wall. However, the cemetery became unprofitable by 1923 and, as some of the graves were closer together than Home Office regulations permitted, the Medical Officer of Health made things worse by getting the City Council to stop further interments except in existing family graves which could be opened.

The company tried to obtain finance to maintain the cemetery but in 1953 went into voluntary liquidation. The Council purchased the cemetery for one shilling in 1957 and was faced with the task of removing grass, weeds, and saplings, which were in some cases higher than the memorial stones. The whole of the work had to be carried without mechanical tools. The lodge and chapels were demolished and the cemetery became a pleasant green space close to the city centre and it also provides a walking route from Canning Circus to Waverley Street, as well as an informal wild life area.

Under the Enclosure Act of 1845 four acres of land were allocated for an Anglican cemetery on Mansfield Road and four acres for additional space for dissenters in the General Cemetery. The site on Mansfield Road, together with other land, was laid out by another proprietary company, which was called the Church Cemetery, but is popularly referred as the Rock Cemetery. This is because the land had, in the past, been used for extraction of sand, which had left hollows and caves. Much work had to be done to form a proper site for burials, but the present appearance is remarkable because of the existence of valleys. There is also a long tunnel with galleries running off which was intended for a catacomb, which did not materialise.

The first burial took place in 1856 and by 1884 44,000 interments were made in nearly 14,000 graves. In 1884 when St Peter's Gate was widened it was necessary to take part of the graveyard of the church. The exhumed remains of 2,000 bodies are buried in 108 graves in a special part of the cemetery. In the hollowed part of St Ann's Valley are a number of horizontal stones with names and ages of children who died in the workhouse. The cemetery can still be used for burials if the proof of ownership of the grave is produced. The cemetery, like the General Cemetery, is now owned by Nottingham City Council.

In 1879 the Borough Council appointed a Public Parks and Burial Grounds Committee. In 1898 the Committee proposed to have two new cemeteries, one at Bulwell and one on Loughborough Road, West Bridgford. These were subsequently opened as the Northern and Southern Cemeteries.

CHÂLETS DE NECESSITE

On 6 December 1880 the Borough Council received a report from the Health Committee, which stated that The Châlet Company Limited, of Thomas Street, London had put forward a proposal. This was that the company would erect a number of 'châlets de necessite', or portable lavatories in convenient places in the town. These would be made of wood, iron and brick, and form

> *a light and pleasing ornament to any thoroughfare. They would have separate compartments, with the necessary furniture, mirrors and all toilet necessaries and under capable attendants. The cost would be a penny for the retiring room and another penny for the lavatory. A shoe black would be in attendance.*

The Council approved the idea, subject to the Health Committee drawing up a proper agreement and deciding upon the situations where the châlets were to be.

The Committee spent the next nine months discussing the details at twelve meetings. It finally considered a proposal to site one of the châlets on Parliament Street but deferred a decision because the Council was considering a major alteration to the town, the construction of a central railway station on the cleared site between Long Row and Parliament Street of some of the worst insanitary houses. The central station never materialised and the châlets were never mentioned again in the Health Committee's meetings.

CHAMBER ESTATE

In 1410 the town of Nottingham appointed officers known as chamberlains, to look after the town's properties. The Chamber Estate was designated as the custodian of these properties to distinguish them from other properties, which the town possessed for special purposes. Eventually these other corporate estates were Bridge, School and Freemen. These properties produced income when let, which could be used for maintenance or improvement, and in some cases for new projects.

When the Corporation became a statutory one under the Municipal Reform Act of 1835, as opposed to its previous Charter corporation, these estates became vested in the new body. In the main the new Corporation's powers were carried out in accordance with Acts of Parliament, but the corporate estates were subject only to common law or in some cases by covenants or trusts imposed by donors. Eventually all the estates were placed under the control of one Estates Committee.

In 1903 the Estates Committee printed a list of all Corporation owned properties running to 289 pages, 282 of which were of three estates. The total of rents receivable was £37,190. The other pages listed the properties of the trading undertakings.

CHAPEL BAR

One of the features of Nottingham, which perplexes strangers, as well as some inhabitants, is that relating to street names. In the original boroughs, where some of today's names go back over a thousand years, a number are called 'gates' rather than streets. This did not mean that they had gates across them, but was a result of the Scandinavian settlers whose language had 'gata' or 'gada', meaning street. On the other hand, the street named Chapel Bar did have a gate as part of a defence against invasion from the north.

Writing in 1749, Dr Charles Deering, author of *A History of Nottingham*, gave a concise account of Chapel Bar, accompanied by an engraving. He described it as the only ancient gate 'which had escaped the injuries of time' until 1743 when it was pulled down. The gateway had two rooms in the shape of pentagons. One of these was a guardroom and the other a chapel for the guards, which gave it the name of Chapel Bar. It had long since, Dr Deering wrote, been used as a brewhouse by Thomas Hawksley, a former Alderman and Mayor of the town, whose house adjoined it. Where several cellars formerly stood, coppers, mash tubs and other utensils filled up the room. Dr Deering said this had resulted in the following lines being written:

Here priests of old turned wafers into God,
And gave poor laymen bread, for flesh and blood,
But now a liquid mystery's here set up
Where priest and layman both, partake the cup.

The name Chapel Bar was also continued as a street name for the small stretch south of the former gate, where in Deering's time were twenty-five houses with 135 residents. Chapel Bar was the main exit from the Market Place to Derby Road until the 1900s. In the 1930s properties on Mount Street and the corner of Chapel Bar were demolished and a new modern cinema, the Carlton, was erected on the site. The shops between Mount Street and Park Row were demolished in the 1960s when Maid Marian Way was completed. New shops were built on Chapel Bar next to the cinema, and

Chapel Bar: the name continued to be given to a short street after the Bar was demolished.

the street was closed to through traffic by a wall. Both the cinema and the shops were demolished in 2001, a new development including a hotel and offices was built on the site, which was renamed the Chapel Quarter.

CHAPELS

The Religious Toleration Act of 1689, which allowed places of worship for denominations other than the Church of England was followed in the eighteenth century by the building of new premises or adapting others for the nonconformist bodies. Although some of these were called churches the practice grew up of referring to them generally as chapels.

Smith and Wild's map of 1820, which covered only the built-up part of the Borough, gave a list of public buildings, which included seventeen chapels. These were described as Baptist, Huntingtonian, Independent, Methodist, Friends Meeting House, Roman Catholic (one small building in Kings Place, Stoney Street), Scandinavian and Unitarian.

When the Borough was extended in 1877, the outer parishes included both Anglican Churches and Nonconformist chapels. *White's Directory* for 1881 listed under 'Non Conformists', details of seventy Wesleyan Methodists, New

Connexion, Congregational, Baptist and Primitive Methodist. A further nine others included Catholic Apostolic Church, New Jerusalem Church (Swedenborgian), Christadelphian Synagogue, Church of the People, (Albert Hall) and Christian Spiritualist.

Listed separately were Roman Catholic, with five churches besides St Barnabas, which it did not describe as a Cathedral although did so in the street list. Friends' Meeting House, St Andrew's Presbyterian, and Jews Synagogue completed the list of non-Anglican churches.

The last *Kelly's Directory* to be published, in 1956, only covered Nottingham and West Bridgford. For the City there were eight Roman Catholic churches, thirteen Baptist, eleven Congregational, one Independent Methodist, nineteen Methodist, one Presbyterian Church of England, six Salvation Army, and one Unitarian. There were also fifteen other places of worship including Catholic Ukrainian, Church of Four Square Gospel, two Church of Christ Scientist, Plymouth Brethren and a Railway Mission Hall.

This was just before the extensive clearance and redevelopments of the remainder of the twentieth century started. This resulted in many of the chapels (as well as Anglican churches) being demolished or closed, with new ones being built in the redevelopment areas in some cases.

CHARITIES

'Charity' has long been a Christian virtue:

And now abideth faith, hope, charity, these three; but the greatest of these is charity.

This was part of Paul the Apostle's first letter to the *Corinthians* and other references to charity are to be found in the Bible.

Prior to the sixteenth century Reformation, the church and religious houses undertook the care of those unable to fend for themselves, either by reason of poverty, infirmity or age. King Henry II in a Charter dated sometime between 1163 and 1174 gave land to the Palmers of Nottingham to establish a hospital for the care of poor men. Hospital in this context was synonymous with almshouse. The hospital was to be established by Robert de Saint Remy 'for the soul of Richard de Saint Remy his brother'.

After the dissolution of the monasteries, wealthy townsmen left wills in which money or rents from land were to be used for charitable purposes. These were often the building of almshouses or for giving goods such as coal to the poor, who were often widows or others with no one to care for them. In his *Annals of Nottinghamshire*, published in 1853, Thomas Bailey in the index to the volumes covering the years up to 1765 lists eighty-eight charities by the names of the founders. These covered the whole county and most of them were founded in the eighteenth century.

The Working Men's Retreat on Plantaganet Street was established by George Gill in 1848 and was retained when much of St Ann's was demolished.

The earliest charity in the Borough was that known as the Agnes Meller's Charity. By this she bequeathed the fortune left by her husband Richard, a bell-founder and one time Alderman and Mayor. This was the foundation of the Free School which in due course, and augmented from other sources, became Nottingham Boys' High School.

White's Directory of 1832 stated that the annual income from Nottingham's bequeathed charities was £3,700 and that other benevolent institutions made similar contributions to, for example, the General Hospital. The directory also gave details of a government commission, which was set up in 1817 to examine all public charities. Its report was not issued until 1830 and was said to have cost £138,850.

Some of the charities provided for payments to be made out of rents of properties, which the benefactors owned. In some cases, where the property was in course of time to become more valuable as a site, they have been able to increase the charitable payments. There are several almshouses in the City which have been erected or improved to modern standards where this has happened. On the other hand Elizabeth Beilby's charity provided for the interest on £20 to be paid to twenty poor widows. This may have been worthwhile in 1697 but with the fall in the value of money would have probably cost more to administer than the interest. In recent years many such small charities have had to be amalgamated or wound up.

CHARTERS

English Boroughs formed in Anglo-Saxon times enjoyed privileges, which the rest of the country did not. The scope of these privileges were set out after the Norman Conquest by charters from the Kings. Nottingham's first one was from King Henry II in about 1160. In it he confirmed a number of rights to levy tolls, which he said the town had assessed in the time of his grandfather, Henry I. He also gave them power to hold markets, to have a monopoly of dyeing cloth within a radius of about nine miles and laid down rules about being a burgess and their property rights.

Each subsequent King issued a new charter usually confirming their predecessor's charters, and some times granting new rights. The Kings were not entirely being generous, as the rights involved paying an annual sum to the King, known as the ferm. Two of the most important of the later charters were those of Edward I in 1284 and Henry VI in 1449. The former gave the burgesses the power to elect a mayor and two bailiffs from amongst themselves. It also allowed them to have a fair lasting fifteen days as well as the one lasting eight days which they already had. The 1449 Charter was even more important as it granted the borough freedom of any jurisdiction of the county. It was described as a corporate county. The Charter also provided that seven Aldermen should be appointed, who were also to be the justices of the peace and one of whom should always be Mayor.

The charters caused a struggle in the second half of the seventeenth century when King Charles II and King James II forced the town to surrender their charters for political reasons and gave it new ones. These were taken back when King William III became monarch and the old ones restored.

A more recent charter was that of Queen Victoria which granted the Borough the status of a City in 1897.

Details of the medieval charters have been printed in the volumes of Borough Records produced by the Corporation from 1882. The first volume included a facsimile of the exact size of Henry II's charter, produced by what must have been an early form of photocopier. Now an even more technological triumph is the production by Nottinghamshire Archives of a CD Rom of the text of the charters, both in Latin and in translation.

CHARTISM

The Reform Act of 1832 which removed the anomalies of Parliamentary pocket and rotten boroughs, with its still very limited voting, did not placate those who wanted a wider franchise. Accordingly, a national movement set out a proposed Charter, from which the term Chartism was derived. This called for six main reforms – universal manhood voting, voting by ballot, payment of members of Parliament, annual Parliaments, equal electoral districts and the abolition of property qualification for members of Parliament.

It was essentially a movement which appealed to the working classes especially as it started at a time of economic hardship. It received an enthusiastic welcome in Nottingham. Large open-air meetings were held at which prominent national Chartists spoke. The prospect of political reform would, it was said, bring about prosperity. A petition to Parliament for its six points to be met was rejected and the movement's activities were curtailed for a while. With further economic downturn and a forceful campaign in Nottingham in which Feargus O'Connor played a leading part, a mass meeting was held on Mapperley Plains in August 1842. Although some said there was no disorder, the Riot Act was read and 400 police arrested a number of men, some of whom were later sent to prison. This was followed by a falling off of Chartism activity, its leaders concentrating on the repeal of the Corn Laws, which were said to be making food for the working classes dearer.

In 1847 the movement re-surfaced and O'Connor was elected as one of the two Nottingham MPs. He was the only Chartist to be elected MP. The following year large protest meetings were planned in Nottingham and London, but the expected number of supporters was not achieved and the meetings passed off peacefully. This more or less meant the end of Chartism. Apart from annual Parliaments, the movement's aims were eventually reached.

☛ *See also Elections, Parliamentary; O'Connor, Feargus*

CHURCHES

In the Domesday Book, compiled in 1086, Nottingham was stated to have a church, on a site which was in the King's lordship. No other details are given but it is almost certain to have been where later the Perpendicular-style church of St Mary was either built or extended from earlier. Nearby, in an archway off Broadway is part of a window from an earlier church, found when excavations to build new lace warehouses were carried out. The Normans later built two other churches, both in the French borough, St Peter's and St Nicholas's. The latter was demolished in the seventeenth century Civil War but was re-built.

The three churches were still the only ones in the borough in 1800. The nineteenth century growth of population and the extension of the Borough resulted in a number of new churches being built so that by 1900, with the churches in the parishes which became part of the borough in 1877, the number had risen to forty-two. The first new one to be built in the nineteenth century was St James's on Standard Hill in 1808, which as an extra parochial district was not then within the borough. This was followed in 1822 by a chapel of ease to St Mary's, St Paul's on George Street. Following an Act of Parliament in 1832, which sought to encourage the building of new churches, there was a continuing stream in Nottingham as new districts were developed. One of these was St Stephen's on Bunkers Hill in 1856 but this was demolished in the 1890s, along with much other property, to make way for Victoria Station for the Great Central Railway. The name was transferred to a new church on Bobber's Mill Road.

The first half of the twentieth century saw a number of the existing churches being demolished such as St James's to provide a site for a nurses' home, and St Thomas's Park Row. New churches built in this period included St Aidan's, Basford, St Margaret's, Aspley and St Faith's, Meadows.

This engraving of St Mary's Church was drawn by the Principal of the School of Art.

The second half of the twentieth century saw a much greater change in the number of churches, mainly due to the large clearance areas in the older parts of the City, especially St Ann's and the Meadows. Here, as elsewhere, some churches were demolished, whilst others became redundant and were used for other purposes. Today, there are thirty-nine church buildings in use for their original purpose.

CINEMAS

The first cinema to be built in Nottingham was on Milton Street and was known as the Victoria Electric Palace. The first performance was on 24 March 1910, the theatre having 450 seats. Moving pictures had been shown earlier but in various premises. A Cinematograph Act had been passed in 1908, requiring proper premises with safety provisions to be licensed by the local authority. Other cinemas known as cinematograph theatres quickly followed in various parts of the City. Until 1929 the films were silent ones, often accompanied by a pianist playing appropriate music.

The advent of the 'talkies' was accompanied by buildings specially designed for the new method, often to a higher standard than previously.

The Elite Cinema is adorned with figures and other decorative features and is a listed building although no longer a cinema.

Some of the 'super' cinemas had restaurants and one in the centre of the City, the Ritz (later named the Odeon) had a Wurlitzer organ, which could be automatically raised and lowered.

By 1939 most people had a choice of cinemas, often within walking distance. The smaller suburban ones usually had a change of programme on Mondays and Thursdays, with afternoon matinees and 'twice nightly' evening performances.

Cinema-going remained popular into the 1950s when television started to be a counter attraction. As a result most cinemas closed and the buildings were used for 'bingo' sessions or for other commercial purposes. Others were demolished and some of the remainder were converted to multi-screen theatres, with a number of small screens giving a choice of programmes. One of these was opened on a new site on the outskirts of the City, but the redevelopment of the former newspaper building on North Sherwood Street resulted in the opening of a new multi-screen cinema in the city centre.

CIVIL WARS

King Charles I started the hostilities, which became known as the Civil Wars between Royalists and Parliament (the Roundheads), at Nottingham on 22

This plaque on Standard Hill was one of a number of Holbrook bequest plaques named after their benefactor.

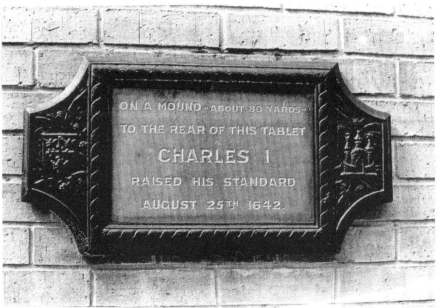

August 1642 by a declaration accompanied by planting a standard on a site near the Castle, which later became known as Standard Hill.

Nottingham, from its central position in England and with a bridge crossing the River Trent occupied a place of strategic importance. The Castle, built as a fortification as well as a royal palace, was taken over by the Parliamentarians, under the governship of Colonel Hutchinson of Owthorpe. This was to cause much inconvenience to the town and its Mayors and Aldermen.

The Royalists had a similar stronghold down the River Trent at Newark and skirmishes took place between the two sides. At one time the Royalists were able to place cannons on the roof of St Nicholas's church, to fire on the Castle. Later, Colonel Hutchinson ordered the church to be pulled down to prevent a recurrence. After 1645, fighting took place in other parts of the country and Nottingham was no longer threatened militarily. After this ended the Castle was demolished by Colonel Hutchinson, and later redeveloped by the Duke of Newcastle.

☛ *See also Castle, The New*

CLEAN AIR

The great increase of the use of coal as fuel, both for domestic heating and for industry resulted in Nottingham having, up to at least until the 1960s, a visible legacy. This was the number of buildings, especially those of light coloured stone, blackened by soot. The smoke was also a health hazard and the Borough Council made bye-laws, as early as 1842, requiring abatement of smoke nuisances. In 1853 the Sanitary Committee complained of

> *increasing nuisances arising from the non-consumption of smoke proceeding from steam engine and other furnaces.*

The Committee had served notices to offending parties but these only had a limited effect. The Committee was particularly annoyed with the Baths and Washhouses Committee

> *setting an example so pernicious as to stop it on the thresh-hold of their endeavours to abate these nuisances.*

In 1868 the Sanitary Committee appointed an Inspector of Nuisances at 30/- (thirty shillings) per week to inspect food and enforce smoke consumption laws.

It was not until the mid-twentieth century that the City Council took more positive steps to prevent smoke nuisance. To start with, it planned the construction of houses on the new Clifton Estate to have fire grates that required only smokeless fuel. It extended this policy to other housing estates where practicable.

The Council's efforts were assisted by the passing of a Government Clean Air Act in 1968. This enabled all local authorities to create smoke-free zones. The Council also embarked on a scheme to encourage owners to clean the soot off some of the more important buildings. 'Operation Clean-Up' was accompanied by offers of financial assistance.

COMMON LODGING HOUSES

On 15 March 1852 the Borough Council received a lengthy report on a letter received from the Government's General Board of Health about a number of matters affecting the town. One of these was that all the common lodging houses had been inspected under a bye-law made in May 1850, to comply with the Common Lodging Houses Act. This also required the Council to make rules for regulating them and for them to be registered.

In its annual report to the Council for the year 1879, the Health Committee stated that it had adopted new bye-laws for common lodging houses, as those adopted nearly thirty years ago were imperfect and unsuited to present requirements. The new rules mainly followed the model bye-laws laid down by the Local Government Board. The rules were printed in full and dealt with the registration of the houses and instructions on keeping them clean and free from disease.

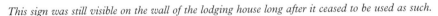

This sign was still visible on the wall of the lodging house long after it ceased to be used as such.

Every window in every room used as a sleeping room had to be fully open for one hour in the morning and another hour in the afternoon. The keeper of the house had to ensure that beds, which had been slept in were not so used again for eight hours. He also had to put up a notice in every room stating the maximum number of lodgers to be allowed.

The largest concentration of the lodgers was in the Narrow Marsh area, where in 1915 there were forty registered houses. When the area was cleared of houses in the 1920s the Corporation was required to erect a new purpose-built hostel, named Sneinton House, to provide accommodation for men displaced from the old lodging houses.

CORONERS

The office of coroner is an ancient one dating back to the twelfth century. He was originally a royal officer whose main task was to maintain the private property of the monarch. Later, from 1230, Nottingham had coroners when the King in a charter gave the borough the power to appoint one. Some of his duties involved hearing court cases and administering oaths but his main role, as it still is, was to enquire into sudden or unexplained deaths. He also has to decide what valuable property unearthed was treasure trove, and also to enquire into shipwrecks (Nottingham does not seem to have many of the latter). Until 1835, he was one of the select body of the Corporation, but under the Municipal Reform Act, the Council elected a suitable person as an officer, paid by fees. The first of these was Michael Browne, in May 1836, who served until his death in 1891. His successor was Charles Lambert Rothera who held the post until 1934. The following two coroners were also of the same family, the latter serving until the 1990s.

The nineteenth century coroners often had to inform the Council of cases of death, which concerned them, especially those of young children.

COUNCIL HOUSE, THE

In 1920, Nottingham, like the rest of Britain, was still suffering from the economic effects of the First World War. Prices and rates of interest were higher than they had ever been, there were shortages of materials for re-building, such as bricks and timber and industrial relations were at a low ebb. Nottingham had one more of a set-back, the rejection by the Minister of Health of its application to extend its boundary. This, the Minister pointed out, was due to its shortcomings in several ways – thousands of dwellings unfit to live in, many without water – borne sewage disposal, inadequate sewage disposal and an antiquated electricity undertaking.

Yet in the next ten years Nottingham was to undergo a radical transformation. A start was made in demolishing unfit and overcrowded dwellings, a new sewage disposal undertaking was created, new roads such as

Under the dome over the Exchange Arcade are four paintings depicting scenes from Nottingham's history.

Valley Road were built as were some 10,000 new houses by the council, with others by private enterprise and a new electricity generating station was constructed as part of the national grid. The Council had acquired both mansion and parkland at Wollaton Hall, and had, with generous help from Jesse Boot, created Lord Trent, built a new University College building in a semi rural situation, with a public park and sports fields flanking a new boulevard. It had also started building new amenities such as libraries, public baths and school clinics.

On top of all this, it moved the old open market from the centre of the City to a new covered market, banished the ancient Goose Fair to the suburbs, demolished the 200 year-old Exchange and built a new Council House and laid out the former market place to match it.

The old Exchange had been only a modest ancillary municipal headquarters since the erection of the Guildhall on Burton Street in 1888 and was surrounded by old shops and public houses. Part of its ground floor was occupied by a meat market, the Shambles. Possibly the last nail in the Exchange's coffin was the realisation that the cost of cleaning these premises exceeded the rents received from them.

The new Council House was designed by architect T C Howitt who had previously been the Council's Housing Architect. The front part contained the council chamber, committee rooms, offices for the civic heads, ballroom and dining room. To the rear was a T-shaped arcade with shops on the ground floor and offices above. It was officially opened in May 1929 by the Prince of

Wales (later King Edward VIII) who, at the dinner which followed pointed out that he was a ratepayer of Nottingham. He owned the Prince of Wales farm on Trent side at Lenton.

There had been much opposition to the scheme, when it was first proposed on the grounds of extravagance at a time of economic stress. Architecturally, it was heavily criticised twenty-five years later by Nikolaus Pevsner in his *Buildings of England* series: 'Nothing much can be said about this kind of Neo-Baroque display' he commented and went on to blame Wren's influence for the dome. Nor did he like the ionic columnation at the front, which supports a highly decorative frieze. He did approve of the shopping mall. He did not mention the painted spandrels immediately beneath the dome, which can be seen by looking up from the arcade. These represent four episodes in the City's history and the faces of some of the men are said to be of the originators of the building.

Pevsner did not mention the two stone lions at the side of the front steps, which have become a much-loved rendezvous point, or the chimes of the clock, named Little John. Today, the Council House is a listed building, and a landmark visible from miles around. It has also achieved more than local fame through television shots, which regard it as a symbol of local government generally.

A newcomer to Nottingham asked what the building was. On being told, it was the Council House, he said he had his name down for one.

☛ *See also Council Houses*

COUNCIL HOUSES

In 1919 the Government passed an Act, which encouraged local authorities to build houses for letting, particularly to members of the armed forces who were being demobilised. The encouragement consisted of an undertaking that if the loss, if any, which occurred by so doing, exceeded the amount of a penny rate, it would be met by means of an Exchequer Grant from the Government. Nottingham City Council took advantage of this by building two large new housing estates, one at Sherwood and one at Stockhill, together with some smaller schemes.

The financial incentive was withdrawn in 1923, but a new form of Exchequer grant was substituted. This provided for payments related to the number of houses built and the Council was required to make a payment, usually one-third of the Exchequer Grant. These arrangements were intended to ensure that the rents that the council charged could be afforded by lower paid tenants who had to be of the working classes. The arrangement also helped the Council to demolish some of the insanitary and overcrowded older houses built by private landlords in the previous hundred years. The outbreak of war in 1939 resulted in the cessation of the building of further council houses and in the demolition of existing houses.

These multi-storey flats at Radford are a completely different type of council dwellings from those in the early years after 1919.

In 1944, in order to encourage Local Authorities once more to provide new accommodation for returning servicemen the Government provided, for those authorities which requested them, pre-fabricated 'temporary' bungalows which could quickly be erected. Nottingham accepted 1,000 of them and had to pay the Government an annual amount to cover the capital cost of the dwellings. It was intended that the bungalows should be demolished after ten years, but because of a continued shortage of rented houses in the City, 'pre-fabs' were retained for up to forty years.

After the war ended in 1945, Nottingham had a waiting list for council houses for families, including once more demobilised troops, of about 12,000 people. Most other towns and cities had a similar problem and the Government again made financial provision for housing authorities to resume building. These included capital grants towards non-traditional, factory-built houses if these cost more than the traditional houses. The Government also insisted that all new council houses should have more modern amenities than were provided in those erected before 1939. Higher subsidies were also provided, as building costs were greater than pre-war and other subsidies were paid for building on more expensive sites and for multi-storey blocks. Until 1954, clearance of older insanitary houses was not allowed. Nottingham had many thousands of such houses and made an early start, especially in those areas where demolition had had to be postponed in 1939.

In the 1960s two major clearance schemes, St Ann's and the Meadows, were started, involving demolition not only of unfit houses, but others as well as shops, factories, even churches, where it was felt necessary to redevelop the cleared sites satisfactorily. These had to be phased over a period of time, of about fifteen years.

Eventually, the number of council houses rose to be the largest sector of houses in the City, at around 60,000. The restriction on only building houses for members of the working classes ceased in 1949, but Nottingham City Council for many years provided houses only for those whom it judged could not afford to buy their own homes. In 1967, the Government by legislation gave council tenants the right to buy the dwelling which they rented and almost half the tenants have done so.

Once the task of demolishing the unfit houses was virtually completed, the need for the Council to build council houses almost disappeared. This was partly due to housing associations taking over a similar role, the increased role of private developers building for sale and, in some cases for rent, and changes in population. These factors meant that one of Nottingham's most unfortunate experiences, the demolition of some 2,500 system-built dwellings, high-rise and deck-access, did not necessitate building new council houses. Those demolished had been built in the late sixties but proved unpopular with tenants and suffered from building defects.

DAIRIES
An Infectious Diseases Act of 1890 gave councils the right to inspect dairies to make sure they were hygienic. Despite this, even in the 1930s, milk sellers used to dispense milk from churns into open jugs. The milk bottle with a sealed top was then a novelty.

DANCING
Dancing of various kinds has a long history going back to pagan times, as well as being associated with religion. An early record of dancing occurs in Nottingham in the Chamberlains' accounts for 1572. Twelve pence was given on 7 June 'unto the daunsers that did gather for a bridge at Clyfton' and a similar amount to 'daunsers that came from Kinoulton'. These were no doubt a form of entertainment and the custom of couples dancing together in an organised way seemed to have arisen in the eighteenth century, particularly on the continent. The increasing gentrification of Nottingham at that time expressed itself in the building of the Assembly Rooms on Low Pavement. Abigail Gawthern who kept a diary covering the last forty years of the eighteenth century made frequent references to balls and dances there, often attended by officers of various Army regiments, which visited the town.

The second half of the nineteenth century with increasing population and manufacturing witnessed a widening variety of public entertainments, including dancing, some of which aroused adverse reactions from some of the largely non-conformist population. In 1889, the magistrates urged the Town Council to obtain Parliamentary powers for licences to be obtained for premises used as a dancing saloon, music hall or concert room. The opportunity arose when the 1890 Public Health Act allowed the council to require annual licences for public dancing, singing, music or other public entertainment. A public meeting presented a petition against such action, which the council ignored.

It was not until the twentieth century that dancing became more available to the ordinary people of the town. A directory of 1920 had no mention of public dance halls, although under the heading 'Dancing and Drill – Professors of' was the Gilmer

Known from the 1920s onwards as the Palais de Danse, one of Nottingham's popular dance halls was called Ritzy for a time until it reverted to part of its original, Palais (but no 'de Danse') name.

School of Dancing. This was followed by the opening of the Palais de Dance in 1925. Music was provided by dance orchestras which were to become widely known through radio and talking films. By 1939 there were other dance halls, including some in the suburbs and eight dancing schools. These were, like cinemas, popular during the Second World War for troops and civilian morale.

In the post-war period, dancing remained popular for some time in the manner exemplified for many years by the BBC's *Come Dancing* programme.

However, the types of dancing changed, clubs open to the small hours replacing the halls of waltz, fox-trot and quick-step.

DANELAW
When the Anglians settled and created the borough of Nottingham, it became part of the kingdom of Mercia, which covered most of the Midlands. To the north was the kingdom of Northumbria occupied by Danes. About AD 860 the Danes captured part of Mercia and created the area known as the Danelaw. This was formed around five boroughs: Nottingham, Derby, Leicester, Stamford and Lincoln. A number of place-names given by the Danes in this area have '- by' and ' – thorpe' elements in them.

King Edward the Elder recovered Nottingham from the Danes and eventually the kingdoms became merged as the English nation. The influence of the Danes in Nottingham is still around, as a number of thoroughfares have 'gate' as part of their name, for instance Fletcher Gate and Pilcher Gate. The 'gate' was derived from a similar word in Danish.

DARRELL, JOHN
John Darrell was born near Mansfield about 1562. He became ordained as a Puritan minister and achieved a certain amount of fame through his activities as an exorcist. The Puritans at this time took literally a biblical reference that exorcism, the airing of people said to be possesed of a devil, could be cured by prayer and fasting.

In 1597 an apprentice in Nottingham, William Somers, was having fits and was said to be possessed by the devil. At the request of the Mayor, Peter Clark, Darrell was asked to exorcise Somers. The fits which Somers had were no doubt epileptic and Darrell claimed that he was possessed of the devil because of the sins of the people of Nottingham and his parents. The Vicar of St Mary had preached for some time about Nottingham's wickedness, until he ceased so doing because other towns were equally wicked.

There was much speculation that further demonstrations of Somers' devil possession whilst suffering fits were inspired fraudulently by collusion between him and Darrell. This led to a prosecution when Darrell was found guilty, deprived of his ordination and sent to prison.

The matter became of some importance because of the established churches stance against the Puritans, leading to a Commission being formed to examine the evidence and in 1630 a Canon of the church prohibited exorcism without a licence from the bishop of the diocese.

DECENNARIES
On 10 April 1308, at the meeting of the Mickletorn (or Great Tourn), the decennaries accused Isolda Arundel of stealing a 'super tunic' and a tunic

with a belt of silver. The decennaries were petty constables, the Latin name for them being *decennarius*. The Mickletorn or Great Tourn was a borough court for minor offences.

When the Hearth Tax Return for 1674 was compiled the inhabitants' names were recorded in thirty sections, each one being described as the 'disnury' of the specified decennaries. The spelling was no doubt the usual way of writing based on hearing the title rather than seeing it written.
☛ *See also Mickletorn Jury; Police*

DEERING, CHARLES, DR

Dr Deering was a German who came to live in Nottingham in 1735 as a medical practitioner until 1749 when he died. After publishing two books, one on smallpox and the other on Nottingham's Flora, he wrote a large history of the town entitled *Nottinghamia Vetus et Nova*. This was not published until four years after his death. It is not a continuous history, but a series of chapters dealing with different subjects. Perhaps the most important parts of the book are his descriptions of life in Nottingham as he saw it, his accounts of the market being particularly vivid.

The book contains a number of engravings, including descriptions and illustrations of the stocking frame and its parts. It is quite appropriate that Deering Street in the Meadows, named after him, should have had until 1970s Jardine's factory for building lace machines. The street has gone but Deering Court perpepuates one of Nottingham's historians.

DEUTSCHER VEREIN

Between 1888 and 1913 the above institution appeared in Nottingham street directories under the heading 'clubs'. It was also mentioned in the street list for 32 Market Street, where it was given the English translation, German Club. About 1904 it had moved to the Poultry Arcade and 32 Market Street was occupied by Kent and Cooper's music shop. The heading 'Clubs' also contained for a short period after 1902 a 'Germania Deutscher Verein', with premises at 8 and 10 St Ann's Well Road.

The Market Street club had as its first chairman Alderman Edward Goldsmith. He had lived in Nottingham since 1851 when as a young man of twenty-four he came from Germany. He became Mayor on two occasions. Another German who came to live in Nottingham in 1836 was Lewis Heymann, who also became an Alderman and Mayor.

The Home Office register of nationalisations has between 1880 and 1900 seventy nationals of various European countries who came to live in Nottingham. Of these, forty-four came from Germany, most of whom formed their own businesses in the town, especially in lace. One of these was Albert Cahn who came to Nottingham in 1873 where he had a furniture business, which prospered and became even more so after he died when his son took over. He was Julian, who became a baronet because of his many charitable benefactions.

The Deutscher Verein no longer appeared in the 1915 *Directory* and must have closed on the outbreak of the First World War. Many of the Germans in Nottingham were interned, leading the Chief Constable to make a scathing attack on those responsible. He said that many of them were elderly, had lived in Nottingham for up to thirty years, some of them having sons serving in the British Army.

The elegant building on Broad Street is now used for National Health purposes.

DIOCESES

Nottinghamshire, including the City, had been part of two dioceses prior to the setting-up of Southwell Diocese in 1888, coterminous with the geographical county. Until 1839 it formed part of the large diocese of York, when, because of increasing population, it was added to Lincoln Diocese.

DISPENSARY, BROAD STREET

In 1831 the Corporation made a donation of £10 to support the setting up of a dispensary in the town. This was done by taking a large house between Hockley and Woolpack Lane, for 'The Nottingham Dispensary for the poor residents in the county and town'. In 1843 it moved to a newly-erected large building on Broad Street, a Corinthian style building. It was to play its part in the treatment of various outbreaks of diseases such as typhus fever, which rapidly spread due to the overcrowded poorer parts of the town, along with the General Hospital and the Workhouse Infirmary.

The Dispensary added General to its title and continued to be part of Nottingham's voluntary medical institution until 1990, when its last report stated that the property on Broad Street was to be taken over by the Area Health Authority.

DISTRICT HEATING

In 1973 the City Council decided to discontinue its method of dumping refuse collected from dustbins. Instead it installed an incinerator, with a tall chimney, at Eastcroft, which was used to provide heat for distribution through part of the City centre for central heating and hot water supply. Parts supplied included St Ann's and the Victoria Centre flats. The administration was carried out in partnership with a private company. Some difficulties occurred at the beginning, mainly in connection with the metering of the supplies, but these were eventually settled.

DOMESDAY BOOK

In 1086 King William dispatched scribes or inspectors to each shire to find out for each one how many adults there were and details of their lands and possessions. The results were written up, in Latin, and have since been translated with explanations. Whilst the primary object was to ensure that proper taxation was levied, the information is the first proper picture of life in England.

As the county town, the borough was described in detail, especially as by 1086, the Anglian or English Borough, had been supplemented by the new French Borough of the castle built by the Normans. It is stated that before 1066 there were 173 burgesses and nineteen villagers and that the tax paid was £18. The tax paid in 1086 was £30, reflecting the addition of the new borough. The town's prosperity was shown by its possession of a mint, which cost it an extra forty shillings in tax, increased to £10 by 1086.

The account gives details of seven Norman landowners, with 134 houses, together with 65 houses in the priest's croft and another 23 houses 'in the ditch' making a total of 222 houses which meant a population of about 1,000 people. The mention of houses 'in the ditch' no doubt refers to the defensive ditch of the original Anglian borough.

The details also informed us that there was a church, which had five and a half acres of land and that William Peverel had ten acres of land for an orchard. The burgesses were quick to point out that they were accustomed to fish in the River Trent but complained that they were forbidden to fish. They, no doubt, hoped that this would be rectified by the King.

EDUCATION, 1870–1902

Prior to 1870, education of children relied on voluntary bodies and religious sources, as set out under 'Academies'.

In 1870 Parliament passed the Elementary Education Act. The object of the Act was to provide for education in schools erected by new bodies, School Boards, with money from government and rates. It was also to make such education compulsory, although this was only to be fully operative later.

School Boards were only to be appointed where there was sufficient local support for one. In Nottingham, the Council were asked by a Workmen's Liberal Union in October 1870 to apply to the Government to appoint one. This was done and an election held for members of the Board. This was fought, not so much on party political grounds, but as between those who objected to schools being paid for out of rates, especially non-conformists, who objected to sectarian Church of England schools receiving grants, and those who favoured education for all.

The School Board erected its first schools in Bath Street in 1874, a building which is still there. It is typical of the other Board Schools erected in the late nineteenth century, tall, with windows too high for the pupils to be distracted by outside events. When the Borough Extension took place in 1877, the School Boards appointed by the other parishes were absorbed into the Nottingham Board. Gradually the limited basic education provided in the early stages was extended to more advanced subjects such as science and woodwork. By the end of the nineteenth century, it had built thirty-six schools and thirty-nine special centres.

In 1902, a new Education Act abolished the School Boards and transferred the duty of administering public education to county councils and county boroughs. Nottingham was one of the latter and so became a Local Education Authority.

Alfreton Road School was one of the School Board's first buildings and still survives as Bentinck Primary School.

EDUCATION, 1902–1918

The City of Nottingham, the title having been added in 1897, already had two major educational institutions, the School of Art and University College, which were administered by the Council. The School Board had also made some provision by 1900 for secondary and high grade schools, but the Boards were not popular with the local councils who had to find money for them from rates.

The Government held enquiries as to the educational requirements for the new century and passed the Education Act 1902. This provided that Local Education Authorities, of which Nottingham as a county borough was one, should have complete control over schools in their area, meeting the expenditure from government grants and its own rates. The control applied to all schools, with provision for sectarian schools to provide religious teaching according to their own beliefs.

Nottingham, with an Education Committee, became responsible for sixty-four school departments (council schools) and fourteen school departments provided by the Church of England and the Roman Catholic Church (trust schools). The pre-war (1914) years were not easy for the Education Committee. Some denominational groups refused to pay part of the rates used for the churches schools, earning the name of 'passive resisters' whose goods were distrained. The Board of Education came down quite hard on the Council because of its lack of resources for building new schools and for repair and improvement of older schools, often leading to overcrowding. It also had to cope with an increase in population and the Council generally was reluctant to spend money in the Edwardian era.

Nevertheless at the outbreak of war, there were two secondary schools, twelve evening institutes, thirty-seven council schools, each with two or three departments and twenty-five trust schools, also with at least two departments. There were also seventeen special centres for handicapped

This classical-style building on Chaucer Street was built in the 1920s as a school clinic. It is now part of Nottingham Trent University.

pupils, technical instruction, handicrafts, physical instruction and centres for providing meals for necessitous children, of which there were six.

There was little that could be done during the 1914–18 war to improve education or schools but in 1918 a new Education Act was passed which sought to reduce the academic gap between elementary and secondary education.

EDUCATION, 1918–1944

The twenty-one years between 1918 and 1939 saw much alteration in education policies, although the improvement in standards required by the 1918 Act proved difficult to achieve. In 1924 however, a significant development was the appointment of the first Director of Education, Mr A H Whipple. Although four existing schools had been designated as central schools, to fill the gap between elementary and secondary schools, the Education Committee adopted Whipple's philosophy. This was based on a scheme of concentrating all phases of education into each of sixteen districts. The late 1920s and 1930s saw much movement of housing from the older inner-city to new outer areas, as a result of clearance areas under the Housing Acts.

This allowed Whipple's system to be applied on the new housing estates such as Aspley, with schools having linked departments, so that pupils progressed in their own areas, through infants, junior and senior departments. The new school buildings were a contrast to the older types, being of one storey only and with French windows. Efforts were also made to encourage community spirit by allowing schools to be used for evening classes and social events such as dances and dramatic societies. Provision was also made for out of school activities for school leavers of fourteen years who had time for such, whilst their unfortunate colleagues at secondary schools were engaged in homework.

Increased secondary school provision was made in 1931 when a new Manning School for Girls was opened. Secondary education was also available outside the local authority system with the two High Schools and the Bluecoat (Church of England) School. The Becket Roman Catholic Secondary School was just outside the city boundary in West Bridgford. There were also twenty-five private schools and several business schools for commercial education.

The City's Education Scheme also initiated open-air schools, at a time when tuberculosis was still prevalent and school clinics with a Senior Clinic Officer and specialists for dentistry and spectacles, for those whose parents could not afford them.

Education suffered a major setback during the Second World War due to evacuation, call-up of staff and requisitioning of some buildings. The future of post-war education was prescribed in the Education Act of 1944.

EDUCATION FROM 1944

The distinction between elementary and secondary education was ended by making education compulsory up to fifteen years and later to sixteen. As after the First World War, new schools were required for the children of parents moving into the new estates, with the City building on average 1,000 new dwellings a year as well as to replace older ones demolished in the vast clearance areas. The Education Act of 1944 provided for primary, secondary and further education. Nottingham established two new technical schools, one for textile trades and the other for the building industry. It also took over part of the former University College Building on Shakespeare Street, as Nottingham and District Technical College, which in a series of changes became Nottingham Trent University. Secondary education, as envisaged in 1944, comprised grammar, technical and modern streams. Nottingham never completely complied with this requirement but later developed bilateral schools and later comprehensive schools. More recently it expanded further education through sixth form colleges culminating in the formation of New College, amalgamating several separate units, under its central prestige building, the former Adams lace warehouse on Stoney Street.

In 1974, local government was reorganised, County Boroughs were abolished and Nottingham became a District Council, along with six others. Major services, including education, became the responsibility of Nottinghamshire County Council. In 1998, the former County Borough, which retained its title of City in 1974, became a Unitary Authority, which meant it resumed those powers, including education, which it lost in 1974.

ELECTIONS – MUNICIPAL

Under the Municipal Reform Act 1835, the first election of councillors took place on 26 December 1835. The town was divided into seven wards, with six councillors in each. The two councillors in each ward with the lowest number of votes had to retire the following November, 1836, and those with the next lowest in November 1837. This was to organise future elections when one-third of the councillors were elected each year.

At a meeting of the Council on 18 January 1836, two of those elected, Dr Payne and J Armitage were members of the Society of Friends and had a conscientious objection to taking the oath required by the Act and their seats were declared vacant. At the same meeting eight new councillors took their

The school at Carrington is typical of the modern buildings erected in the post-war era.

seats having been elected at by-elections. These were caused by the Council having elected fourteen Aldermen, eight of whom had been elected as councillors in December 1836. The remaining six had been elected by the Council, mainly men who had held office in the old Corporation. The Council could elect as aldermen either from councillors or from others who were eligible to be elected as councillors. Thereafter, it was only on two or three occasions that aldermen were elected who were not councillors.

Aldermen were elected for a term of three years, but the seven who had received the most votes served for six years in the first instance. At the 1840 election, the two councillors elected for Park Ward were declared to have been elected improperly, as there was no presiding alderman present at the election. A subsequent election took place for the two seats in Park Ward.

The former Whigs, now known as Liberals, were always in the majority until 1906, although on one occasion in the 1840s, the Conservatives won nearly enough seats to gain control. This was due to the intense struggle over the proposal to erect a new workhouse.

At the first municipal election after the passing of the Ballot Act 1872, there were sixty-five nominations for the fourteen seats. In Park Ward and in St Ann's Ward there were thirty-seven nominations. At this election two candidates received the same number of votes, so the Mayor gave his casting vote in favour of one of them. In the following January, an independent inquiry was held to hear allegations about bribery. The two members for St Ann's Ward, R A Sylvester and J Hartshorn, were found to have been guilty of treating. Their elections were declared void and Sylvester ordered to pay costs of £2,500.

At the subsequent by-election, Hartshorn was elected together with J Sylvester, brother of the former councillor. The other two candidates were W Pyatt and W Pare. However, there were thirty-three other nominations, most of which were frivolous in false names of the four candidates. Steps were taken legally to prevent such happenings.

After the Borough was extended in 1877 to bring in surrounding parishes, the number of wards was increased to sixteen, with only three councillors, one of whom retired each year. The number of aldermen was also increased to sixteen. Similar adjustments were made in the twentieth century after the more limited two further extensions.

In 1974, Nottingham ceased to be a County Borough, which it had been since 1888 when such boroughs were made independent of the new County Councils created by the same. From 1974 to 1998, Nottingham became a District Council with some of its major functions transferred to the County Council. In 1998 these powers were handed back to the City when it was granted 'unitary' status. The office of Alderman was abolished in 1974 but the City Council has appointed as honorary aldermen former councillors and aldermen. Their duties are mainly ceremonial and they play no part in administration.

☛ *See also Guardians, Nottingham Board of*

ELECTIONS, PARLIAMENTARY

History is essentially the story of change over a period of time. England, and Nottingham, saw great changes in both the eighteenth and nineteenth centuries, which can be measured to some extent by the Parliamentary elections. A significant change, which may or may not be readily assessed as to its effects, was the change from open voting, with the names of the electors and for whom they voted published, to secret voting by ballot. The latter came about in 1872 by the Ballot Act.

The first General Election under the new method was on 4 February 1874 and the Nottingham Date Book recorded that there was not the amount of excitement at the various polling places. There were four Liberal candidates, none of whom were elected because of the split vote, leading the two Conservative candidates being elected for the two seats.

The Date Book went on to say that after dark, a great body composed of the lowest class, mainly young men, paraded the principal streets, breaking windows of warehouses, offices, public buildings and private houses. Many street lamps and those on Trent Bridge were damaged.

A hundred years earlier the only excitement at the election was the appearance of a soldier wearing a sword. The crowd would not let him into the polling booth until he drew his sword, waving it about, hitting one person. He then forced his way in and refused to come out. The crowd thereupon brought the polling to halt until the Mayor arrested him and broke his sword in two. Elections in the eighteenth century were mainly uneventful as the Corporation with its control through the creation of burgesses could ensure that, by agreement, the two seats were usually held by one Tory and one Whig.

The nineteenth century was to see a very different picture especially after 1832, when the qualification for voting lessened the burgess's influence. The town was to suffer periodic bouts of unemployment because of fashion changes in the textile trades, the frame-knitters were badly paid and there was a much greater reaction from working men seeking better times. In the 1840s the Chartist movement was active and in Nottingham a proposal to build a new workhouse was unpopular.

This former landmark on Greyfriar Gate was the Walter Fountain which commemorates the election as MP for Nottingham, in 1846, of John Walter, a proprietor of The Times. *It was demolished to make way for the Broad Marsh Centre.*

Bribery and corruption had also been prevalent but 'Nottingham Lambs' became notorious for the violence and intimidation.

At the 1841 election each party had hired gangs of 'Lambs' which at one stage met in a pitched battle, with fists, sticks and stones wrapped in handkerchiefs being used. On hearing of this, a number of country gentlemen mounted on horses harried the gangs until the 37th Dragoons appeared. The two successful candidates were G G Larpent and Sir John Hobhouse, both Liberals. John Walter, the owner of *The Times* newspaper, stood as a Tory but was defeated. The election was, as usual, accompanied by riotous behaviour and payments and drink supplied to voters.

The following year, allegations were made that supporters of Larpent, now Sir George Larpent, had made illegal payments of which he was unaware. As a result Sir George said he would retire and not oppose John Walter at the by-election. In the event the Liberals refused to abide by the arrangement and opposed Walter who, however, was elected, but only by a small majority.

The 1847 election was even more remarkable. John Walter, one of the two MPs did not stand but his son was nominated, without his consent, and was elected whilst the other seat was won by Feargus O'Connor, the Chartist leader. He was the only chartist to be elected as an MP. John Walters was commemorated by the erection of the Walter Fountain in Greyfriar Gate, but it was pulled down to make way for the Broad Marsh Centre. A statue of Feargus O'Connor was erected in the Arboretum where it still stands.

ELECTRICITY

Electricity can be produced by chemical, mechanical and frictional means, but it was not until 1832 that Michael Faraday produced a dynamo which paved the way for mechanically produced electricity to be generated on a commercial scale. In 1882 the Government passed the Electricity Act, which gave local authorities and companies powers to set-up electricity undertakings. Nottingham Corporation already had two utilities, gas and water, which it had purchased from private companies. There was surprisingly little enthusiasm from private companies to start electricity undertakings, as after twenty-one years they could be purchased compulsorily by local authorities.

Nottingham Corporation established a committee to consider having such an undertaking and nine years later finally decided to do so. Such a novelty naturally called for proper investigation and this was not really encouraging from one source. This was Thomas Hawksley who had been born in Arnold and became Nottingham's Water Engineer, until he moved to London to become a consulting engineer. In a report he claimed that it could never

The first electricity generating station on Talbot Street was demolished to make way for a hotel and car park.

become as useful an illuminant as gas. He stated that it would have a place for peculiar and exceptional purposes:

> *Gas is a docile animal which you may place in anyone's charge, whilst electricity is an untameable wild beast which must always be kept under special and even scientific control.*

Having taken the decision to embark on such a dangerous mission, it took three years for the Corporation's generating station and cable network to be completed, in 1894. The station was on Talbot Street and used coal-fired boilers to drive the dynamos. These produced direct current, in the same way as from batteries and accumulators. It was to be many years before AC (alternating current) was produced with its much greater scope.

The area of supply was limited at first to premises in and around the city centre. In the first full year the maximum demand was only 255 kilowatts and did not reach 1,000 kilowatts until 1899. By 1914 the demand had risen to nearly 7,000 kilowatts. Some of this increase was due to the Corporation's tramways using electricity from 1902. To facilitate this, a further generating station was built at the bottom of St Ann's Well Road. One problem was that unlike gas electricity could not easily be stored. This was overcome by installing large accumulators, which could be charged at night time when the trams were not running.

During the First World War, Cammell Lairds built a munitions factory in the Meadows and the Electricity Department made special arrangements to supply the additional electricity required. After the war a large new modern station was erected at North Wilford. In 1926 this became part of the national grid of electricity stations, which by interchange facilities could meet demands at different times throughout the country.

The 1930s saw a great expansion in Nottingham's electricity undertaking, its area of supply extending outside the City boundaries. The use of electricity by 1939 was practically universal both for industry and domestic residences. Houses were assisted to change from gas by spreading the initial cost of wiring and by collecting the charges by pre-paid meters. The undertaking also sold appliances such as cookers, fires and water heaters.

In 1947, under the Electricity Act, the City Electricity Department, like all other undertakings, became nationalised and became part of the East Midlands Electricity Board.

EMIGRATION

In 1820 Nottingham was experiencing one of its frequent slumps in the hosiery trade, which relied to some extent on meeting changes in fashion. The frame-working knitting industry was declining because of competition from powered factories in the north of England. Wages were low and there was no chance of obtaining alternative sources of employment. One way of relieving some of this poverty was the result of a committee being set-up to organise emigration of those willing to go to Cape Colony in South Africa. The committee was chaired by the Duke of Newcastle who gave £500 towards a relief fund, which reached £4,000. Three hundred people from the town took advantage to go there, along with others from the county.

Less willing emigrants, to Australia, were those transported there as punishments for crimes. More volunteers did however undertake to emigrate to Australia, New Zealand, Canada and the United States of America. Some of these were undertaken by private decisions of individuals, often those who had particular skills of use to the countries to which they went. Others went as part of organised schemes. One of these was organised in the 1860s by Nottingham nonconformists who were settled in a part of New Zealand known as the Albertlanders.

After the First World War efforts were made in Nottingham to encourage emigration as a means of countering unemployment, a meeting being held in March 1929 at the University College, Shakespeare Street, to discuss migration within the Empire. Similarly, after the Second World War emigration to Australia was encouraged by assisted travelling costs.

ENCLOSURE

From the middle ages onwards, enclosure was the process by which the agricultural systems, in the central part of England in particular, were altered. Most villages in Nottinghamshire had the open field system whereby two or three large fields were cultivated on the strip method. Each tenant (most of the fields and lands were owned by wealthy and aristocratic families) was allocated a number of strips, which were usually separated from each other, so that each man did not have the best or the worst lands. For a number of reasons this gradually became regarded as wasteful and uneconomic.

Enclosure in these circumstances meant the end of the old strips and the open fields. Instead, fields as we know them today (or did until recently) were

One of the provisions of the 1845 Enclosure Act was the making of the Arboretum in the Sandfield.

Another provision in the Act was a tree-lined walkway in the Clayfield of which Elm Avenue was a part.

allocated to tenants, surrounded by hedges and often with new roads for access to them. This, the so-called Agrarian Revolution, was accompanied by new crops and more scientific husbandry. To achieve this pattern, some owners of land could carry it out by agreement, but many others had to be sanctioned by an Act of Parliament.

In Nottingham, the term 'enclosure' began to be the subject of controversy in the eighteenth century. Nottingham did have open fields from Anglo-Saxon times, but as it became an urban market town and later an industrial one, the situation was somewhat different. The medieval structure consisted of ownership and use of the fields being enjoyed in common by the burgesses. They became united as a body with a mayor, aldermen, sheriffs and other offices who were responsible to the principal inhabitants, the burgesses.

By the end of the eighteenth century, the population had tripled to nearly 30,000 compared to 10,000 thirty years earlier. Most of the increase was due to people coming to live in Nottingham from elsewhere, attracted by the growing textile trades, based on the stocking-frame. They were not usually burgesses and the latter were unwilling to see the common lands built on, as they would lose their rights of access, which were valuable. Even if the burgesses did not farm themselves, they could let their rights for money. This had the effect of the older inhabited part of the town becoming more and more built on, with often shoddily built houses in overcrowded courts and alleyways.

This was to lead, by the 1840s, to Nottingham becoming described as one of the worst slum areas in Britain. Agitation for the open fields to be built on was started by more socially conscious inhabitants as early as 1797 but the unelected corporation successfully opposed enclosure. It was not until after the Municipal Reform Act 1835 resulted in an elected borough council that enclosures were allowed by Acts of Parliament. The first, a small one, in 1838 was known as the Lammas Field enclosure to the north of Park Row. The main act in 1845, a General Enclosure Act, allowed the remaining open fields, the Sandfield, the Clay Field and the Meadows, to be developed. (Enclosure was usually spelt 'inclosure')

EVACUATION

The word 'evacuation' came to have a special meaning in 1939. It was applied to a scheme formulated by the government for the removal, mainly of children, from areas of Britain to what was regarded as safer places, than those in populous areas, in the event of air raids or invasion of enemy forces.

What became known as 'official' evacuation was planned in early 1939, when Nottingham City Council appointed an Emergency Committee to plan ahead to meet eventualities if war broke out, as it did in September 1939. The Government had already established a North Midlands Region, with wide powers, to oversee the preparations as these involved co-operation of the City Council with other local authorities and with the transport and military authorities.

Basically the scheme provided for the defining 'evacuation' areas from which children were thought to be at risk and transferring them to safer, usually more rural and less highly populated districts, known as 'reception' areas. The main task of organising the actual transfer of the children was for them to be dealt with from schools, with teachers acting as escorts.

The Nottingham 'evacuation' area was less in extent than the City, and included mainly the older, more densely populated areas, and excluded for instance such suburbs as Wollaton and Sherwood, as well as most of the newer parts where large council estates had been built. This necessarily somewhat arbitrary division led to the situation in May 1941, when the heaviest air raid took place on Nottingham, that the bombing, made easier by the River Trent, was concentrated on both sides of the river. The north side was an evacuation area whilst West Bridgford on the south side was not.

Within three days of the outbreak of war some 4,000 children had been evacuated from Nottingham. Evacuation was not compulsory and parents had the difficult decision as to whether families should be broken up, if the under school age children stayed whilst their siblings were evacuated. The other side of the coin was what the evacuated children would be treated like in the homes to which they were sent.

In recent years, books, radio and television programmes have described, from reminiscences, some of the experiences of those evacuated, as well as from those who acted as parents.

By March 1940, as no major war action had taken place, a period known as the 'phoney' war, many of those evacuated returned home. After the invasion of the Low Countries by Germany, and the withdrawal of British armed forces from the continent, Britain faced a new threat of heavy air raids. As a consequence some evacuation again took place. Not all of this was 'official', as parents if they could, made their own arrangements.

In June 1944, the Allied Forces invaded France in what was to prove to be the beginning of the end of the European war. Germany retaliated in a fresh attempt to intimidate the English civilian population by launching unmanned missiles over London and South East England. This resulted in large numbers of people, mainly women and children, leaving the affected areas for safer parts.

Nottingham was declared a reception area, thus reversing its earlier evacuation policy. By August 5,703 people had been sent to Nottingham where arrangements were made to receive them in rest centres and then find accommodation for them. As the V1 and V2 rockets were no longer effective by November 1944, as the Allied Forces pushed the German Army eastwards, most of these refugees were able to return home. At the same time those Nottingham children who had been evacuated to reception areas were allowed to return home.

EXCAVATIONS

Until about the eighteenth century, most houses in Nottingham were built without deep foundations. When they became worn out they were taken down, earth would be spread over the site and new buildings built on top of it. From the eighteenth century onwards more substantial new houses were built which required deeper foundations. Similarly, when warehouses and industrial buildings were built, a similar situation arose. In both cases any traces of what had previously been on the site were probably destroyed.

When the Lace Market was created from about 1850 onwards, the new large warehouses would excavate, often with a view to incorporating cellars. Again in most cases, no record as to what was there before, was made.

About thirty-years ago Halifax Place Methodist Chapel was demolished to make way for a new housing development. Adjoining the chapel site was what had for many years been a garden or orchard. When excavation for the new foundations were started, it was revealed that the site had been occupied for over a thousand years and traces of occupations at different periods were discovered. A survey was carried out by the City Archaeologist and important artefacts from the Danish period of settlement were found. In the days before refuse collection was organised it was the usual practice to discard broken crockery and similar items by burying them in pits and from these the archaeologists were able to estimate the various periods of occupation of this site.

This of course was not the first archaeological inspection made and in the late nineteenth century some opportunities arose for such when road widening or demolitions took place. There was a growing awareness of the importance of such opportunities and the Thoroton Society of Nottinghamshire was founded in 1897 to support such interest. The twentieth century has provided many occasions when archaeological surveys have given valuable insight into Nottingham's history. There has been a statutory obligation for some time that developers of sites, which may yield information, allowing surveys to be carried out.

EXECUTIONS

The earliest recorded execution in Nottingham was in 1212, when King John ordered a number of Welsh hostages to be hanged from the castle walls because the Welsh had broken the conditions relating to the hostages.

Along with bear-baiting, cock-fighting and public whipping, executions were regarded as a spectacle to be watched or even enjoyed. In a period of twenty-one years, from 1832 to 1860, six publications were issued in Nottingham, giving 'correct lists of executions' which had taken place over the previous 700 years. A later list ran through eight editions bringing the

The small square block on the second step could be lifted out to take a pole of the scaffold outside the Shire Hall.

story up to 1923. The publication of newspapers from the early eighteenth century onwards gave full details of those occasions.

An Act of Parliament in 1752 required those sentenced to death to be executed the following day and their bodies to be given to surgeons for dissection. The first execution in Nottingham after the Act was passed took place on Gallows Hill, Mansfield Road, where later St Andrew's Church was built. The victim was James Wogden, a man of fifteen stones who resolutely refused to get out of the cart in which he was taken to the gallows. The executioner had to fasten a halter round him and dragged him up.

It was the custom to allow those to be hanged to take a drink at the *Nag's Head* nearby before being hanged. On one occasion the murderer refused to take a drink. Had he done so he would have lived as a pardon arrived just after he was hanged.

Later hangings were carried out by a scaffold, which had been erected each time on the steps of the Shire Hall. On 8 August 1844, William Saville was hanged there in front of an immense crowd, which packed the narrow street. After the execution, fourteen people died and hundreds of others injured when panic broke out as people tried to escape.

Despite this, public executions were still carried out up to 1864, but later they were done inside prisons. By 1928, (the last execution in Nottingham) there had been 134, 104 of which took place in the eighteenth and nineteenth centuries. Some of those in the eighteenth century were for burglary and highway robbery, but later were always for murder.

EXTENSION OF BOROUGH AND CITY

In 1877 an Act of Parliament brought within the borough boundaries the following villages or parishes – Basford, Bulwell, Lenton, Radford, Sneinton, North Wilford and the liberties of the Castle, Brewhouse Yard, Standard Hill and the Park.

From 1 April 1932 the City boundaries were extended by Act of Parliament mainly to bring within the City adjoining lands where the Council had started to build council houses under the Housing Acts from 1919. These were at Bilborough, Wollaton, Bestwood (part) and small areas of Colwick, Strelley and Beeston.

Several of these markers were put up to show the extended City boundary in 1933.

From 1 April 1952, the City boundaries were again extended, to its present limits, by taking in Clifton and South Wilford. At the same time, a minor anomaly in the boundary between the City and the County around Trent Bridge was altered by making the centre of the River Trent the dividing line.

FAIRS

Nottingham as a borough from Anglo-Saxon times had been, like other English towns, a market town for the surrounding countryside. From markets developed annual fairs, which in the autumn enabled the country people to sell their surplus harvest produce and also to stock up for the winter with such things that they could not produce themselves. After the Normans came, fairs became formally recognised by Royal Charters. This gave

The Town Clerk, Mr P M Vine, is seen here reading the proclamation to open Nottingham's famous Goose Fair.

the borough rights to levy tolls, for which privilege they had to pay fees to the Royal Exchequer.

In a charter of 1284, Edward 1 granted permission to Nottingham to hold a second fair, thus showing that the existing one was older than 1284. He did stipulate that this was not to damage neighbouring fairs. Nottingham had such a neighbour, the fair held at Lenton. About 1300 the Prior and Convent made an agreement with the borough to settle a difference, which had arisen. As a result Lenton curtailed its own fair by four days so that Nottingham did not face competition. This agreement also gave some interesting sidelights about Lenton fair. Cloth merchants, apothecaries, pilchers (glove makers) and mercers from Nottingham could hire booths at Lenton for twelve pence. The booths measured eight feet in length and eight feet in width.

Nottingham's October fair became known as Goose Fair in the sixteenth century, farmers from some distance away from Nottingham driving flocks of geese to be sold. The fair retained its trading character until the nineteenth century when the pleasure fair, which it still is, grew in importance. By the

1920s its tenure of the Old Market Place ended, when a new central market was opened and the fair moved to the Forest Recreation Ground.

FAMINE

Today, the word 'famine' is usually thought of as something that affects undeveloped countries in the third world. Seven hundred years ago, Nottingham was to suffer famine, as part of what became known as the 'Great European Famine of 1315 to 1317'. It started to rain on 11 May 1315 and did not stop the whole of the summer and into autumn. The Trent overflowed its bank, damaging its bridges and nearby roads. The effect on crops was catastrophic, particularly corn, which was the main crop, providing bread. Such wheat as survived was of poor quality and of course the price of bread rose reaching prices ten times more than it was earlier.

The effects of this were described in the *Nottingham Date Book*. Children were said to have been stolen and eaten, whilst new prisoners entering jails were torn to pieces by the inmates for food. Nottingham and the rest of the agricultural county suffered as much as anywhere. Fortunately the land soon recovered in 1317, but one unsavoury aspect of the famine was that a few were able to take advantage by hoarding stocks of corn and making substantial fortunes.

FARMER – A MUSICAL FAMILY

In 1853, W H Wylie in his book *Old and New Nottingham* wrote 'John Farmer, a popular glee singer, has for a long period of years been a favourite in Nottingham and the Midland Counties'. He added 'his son Henry is decidedly the first musician in Nottingham at the present time'. He went on to mention his compositions, his conducting oratorios and his violin playing.

John died in 1874 aged eighty-three, having been the landlord of the *Crown and Cushion* public house on Weekday Cross, which was said to be very popular for its concerts, especially at Goose Fair.

Henry also had a brother John. He had a wholesale milliner's business where he also lived in 1851. He was married with six children aged between seven and fifteen, with four living in assistants and two servants. The eldest child was John, fifteen and his sister Mary was thirteen. Both these were to have long careers connected with music. John worked in his father's business until 1857, but from 1864–85 he was music master at Harrow School and then from 1885 until 1901, when he died, organist at Balliol College, Oxford. Whilst at Harrow he composed the school song.

Mary also had a second forename, Hutton, and married in 1857 Thomas George Bowman, son of a Nottingham wine merchant. In 1861 she was living at Colville Street, her father's house which he had moved to when he ceased to be a milliner and became a lace manufacturer. Mary was twenty-

PIANOS.   ORGANS.   VIOLINS

HENRY FARMER & CO.,

Pianoforte and Organ Dealers

HIGH STREET, NOTTINGHAM.

The Finest Selection of UPRIGHT & GRAND PIANOS in the Cit

Henry Farmer & Co. are SOLE AGENTS for—
STEINWAY PIANOS.
BROADWOOD PIANOS.
KNAKE PIANOS.
ECKE PIANOS.
SCHIEDMAYER PIANOS.

Large Discount for Cash
—⚬⚬—
All Instruments may be had on the
EASY PAYMENTS SYSTEM.

HENRY FARMER & Co.'s **TUNERS** visit every part of the County, and all Orders are promp attended to.

REPAIRING PIANOS AND ORGANS.—HENRY FARMER & Co. give Estimates free for kinds of Repairs, which are done entirely on the premises by first-class workmen.

HENRY FARMER & CO., Piano and Organ Showroom

Telephone 516.   High Street, NOTTINGHAM.

Henry Farmer and Company moved to Long Row West where the business remained until the 1980s.

three and married but her husband's name was not shown in the census return. She evidently worked for her father as a superintendent. Ten years later she was still living at Colville Street but was a widow, occupation music teacher. In 1879 she was married a second time, to Charles Hart, fourteen years her junior, a lace manufacturer. Mary then became known as Mary Hutton Bowman Hart (sometimes hyphenated), her second husband dying in 1884.

Mrs Bowman Hart, in addition to other teaching appointments, was music mistress at Nottingham Boys' High School. She also ran a music school in Nottingham known as the Harrow Music School. This was at 52 Long Row and seems to have been in conjunction with her brother, John, as it was described as the Nottingham Branch. She also spent a great deal of time in social work and writing 'improving' literature.

FARROWS BANK LIMITED

An advertisement for this bank appeared in *White's Directory* for 1920. It had two branches in Nottingham, one on Milton Street and another on Radford

Road, Hyson Green. It is to be hoped that not many Nottingham people put money in the bank as on 20 December 1920 the bank suspended payment. The following January a compulsory winding up order was made. At a subsequent court hearing it was stated that the business of the bank had been incompetently managed by the board of directors. There was a deficiency of £2¹/₂ million and for some years the bank had submitted accounts showing profits when in fact losses had been incurred. Even income tax had been paid on the non-existing profits. The chairman, seven directors and the auditor were summoned for misfeasance.

The bank had been started by Thomas Farrow and William Walter Crotch and had thirty-seven provincial branches.

This advertisement appeared in 1902 at a time when the directors were aware of the financial position.

FELKIN, WILLIAM

The author of *A History of the Machine-wrought Hosiery and Lace Manufactures* was born at Ilkeston, Derbyshire, in 1795. He was the son of the Reverend William Felkin, a Baptist minister with a large family who nevertheless managed to give him a good education. William junior, in his book wrote that he entered the stocking-making business in 1808 and the lace trade in 1819. He also paid tribute in his book to the help he received from his grandfather, also William, who was a stocking-maker at Bramcote. He was also, through his connections with the Nottingham firm of Heard and Hurst, to obtain a post for his grandson with the hosiery firm. He later became acquainted with John Heathcoat, who had patented a lace machine, which was to result in the growth of the Nottingham lace trade.

William Felkin became a lace manufacturer in Nottingham, at first in partnership with William Vickers and later with his son but this business collapsed in 1864. He also spent a great deal of time compiling statistics of the textile trades, addressing meetings and giving evidence to inquiries. In so doing he was able to acquire the detailed knowledge to write a 559-page book.

Despite all this he also managed to find the time to serve on the Nottingham Council as a Councillor for Park Ward from 1846 to 1856, when he was made an alderman, an office he held until 1868.

A centenary reprint of his book was issued in 1967, which contains more information about Felkin, written by Professor S D Chapman along with an index.

FREEMEN

Known as burgesses until 1835, the freemen of Nottingham were able to secure some of their ancient rights under the Municipal Reform Act of that year. This was followed by two local Acts, which started the building on the former common fields and under which the lands were allocated to new owners, and the freemen obtained considerable allotments. These were vested in a Freemen's Estate, regulated by a Freemen's Committee. The income

FREEMEN

The "FREEMEN'S COMMITTEE talk of SELFISHNESS,—

Who stopped CRICKET PLAYING in t Meadows?

Who corruptly countenance the erection Manure Yards in Lee's Close, alrea the most sickly part of the Town?

Who rake Manure off the Land, and se it?

Who make demands and exactions and exe cise the influence of Terrorism, and r sort to Club Law?

Who seized the Parish Farm, and Fore Stallage?

Who seek to Enclose Mapperley Hill, a the Forest?

Who attempt to control and overawe th Town Council?

Nottingham, Feb. 3, 1845.   J. SHAW, PRINTER

The freemen were not regarded with approval by some of the town's other inhabitants.

These houses were erected on Canning Circus with funds arising from the compensation for the loss of freemen's rights.

from the estate was used to pay sums of money, known as Freemens' Annuities to freemen and their widows.

In 1882 the Corporation obtained an Act of Parliament, which transferred all the lands and payment of annuities to it. This was used to put an end to the creation of new freemen and for the gradual cessation of the annuities as the existing freemen and their widows died. A new Freemen's Committee was set up consisting of seven members of the council and six freemen. The committee had to satisfy itself that all payments of the annuities went to those qualified to receive them.

On 23 May 1980 the last meeting of the Freemen's Committee took place. It was reported that Thomas Shepperson Sewell had died on 12 March 1980, aged ninety-eight. He was the last surviving recipient of a Freemen's annuity and the Committee was no longer required.

FRIARS

Two orders of friars were established in Nottingham in the thirteenth
century. The first one was the Friars Minor or Grey Friars, extant in 1230.
The order had established itself in England in 1224. Their house was at the

This is a conjectural plan of the Carmelite Friary.

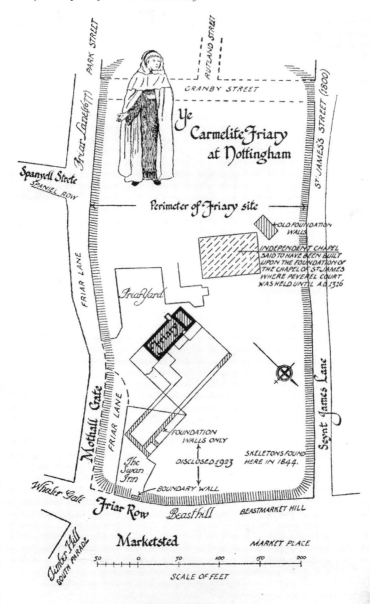

west end of Broad Marsh and later Greyfriar Gate was named after them. One of the heads of the order was William of Nottingham, being here from 1240–54. After the murder of King Richard II, the order was involved in the unrest nationally and two of the Nottingham orders were arrested and imprisoned in the Castle. Some of the friars were executed and the mayor ordered the head of one of them to be mounted on the Castle walls.

The Carmelites or White Friars were known to be in Nottingham before 1271 when the King gave them protection. Their friary was on a central site between Moothall Gate and St James Street. The *Bell Inn* nearby is said to have taken that name because the angelus bell could be heard there. Angel Row was similarly named after the bell. Moothall Gate was re-named Friar Lane and Beastmarket Hill was formerly known as Friary Row.

The orders were mendicant ones and do not appear to have been too popular in Nottingham for this reason. The orders were disbanded by the Reformation.

GAS

In 1818 the earliest gas works were established in Butcher's Close and Island Street, off London Road, where today the Island complex is being built. It was started by the Nottingham Gas Light and Coke Company. By 1819 lamps had been erected on Hollowstone, Drury Hill, Bridlesmith Gate and

This is all that remains of the former Gas Works at Basford.

six in the Market Place, a total of ten. This innovation was not universally popular, as people thought that as the pipes leading from the works to the lamps were laid beneath the streets, they might get their feet burned.

A retort house was built, 34-feet by 22-feet, and gas was produced by heating coal and siphoning off the gas to a holder. The stokers were paid 20s (shillings) and 6d (sixpence) for 8 months and 25s (shillings) for 4-months, presumably in the winter months. The process resulted in a residue of coke, which could be sold and also various chemicals. Tar was widely used for putting on the timbers of older houses, which previously had been brown in colour. Thus the concept of black and white half timbered houses only dates from this time.

The business grew and eventually extended to industrial use in gas engines. The company extended to new works at Radford, Basford, Eastcroft and a chemical works at Giltbrook, near Kimberley. The Company was taken over in 1874 by Nottingham Corporation, which continued to expand its supply to a wide area around the City. Under the Gas Committee it became a valuable asset to the City, as its profits were used to reduce the general rates.

From 1 May 1949, the Corporation ceased to own the undertaking, which under the Gas Act 1948, was transferred to the nationalised East Midlands Gas Board. The wheel took a further turn in the 1970s when the nationalised boards were sold off. British Gas issued shares in the new company, in a well-publicised publicity campaign featuring the phrase 'If you see Sid, tell him'.

GAWTHERN, ABIGAIL

Born Abigail Anna Frost in 1757, she married Francis Gawthern, her cousin, in 1783. She was comparatively wealthy herself, having annuities worth £6,705 when she married. Her husband's father and grandfather had businesses in Nottingham, which Francis inherited along with properties including their home at the corner of Drury Hill and Low Pavement, a handsome large building.

Abigail had been educated at a Nottingham private school until she was ten, when she went to a boarding school at Clapham. When she returned to Nottingham her social education continued with lessons in music, riding and dancing, and with visits to fashionable resorts. She lived to the age of 65. In 1822 when she died she had lived through a period of great change in Nottingham, seeing it become an industrial town from a pleasant mainly new eighteenth century one of a population only a quarter of its size.

She started to write up a journal or diary in about 1808, but this dated back to 1751 and was transcribed from earlier pocket books. It is mainly a chronological record of various happenings, personal and public with many references to middle and upper class people and some of the more important incidents in Nottingham. The diary has been transcribed and published by The Thoroton Society of Nottinghamshire, with an index.

There are thirteen references to dancing and forty-one to balls and assemblies. Under public events are balloon ascents, circuses, firework displays, illuminations, menageries, theatre and drama. More serious subjects were riots, executions, funerals and medical treatment. A great number of personal references refer mainly to the gentry class, some of whom were known to her. Her references are not all flattering. On 17 March 1804, for example, she noted 'Mr John Huthwaite died in London: a worthless character'.

GEORGIAN NOTTINGHAM
In his book *History of Nottinghamshire* (1947) Professor A C Wood wrote that the fortunate minority in Georgian England enjoyed a graceful stately life. It was accompanied in Nottingham, as elsewhere, by a large re-building of parts of the borough by houses mainly of brick in an ordered style known as Georgian architecture. The building by the Duke of Newcastle of his new mansion on the site of the old castle led to an influx of wealthier gentry who could afford the new houses erected in Castle Gate, Hounds Gate, Low, Middle and High Pavements, some of which still remain.

In addition to this physical background the Georgian period saw Nottingham becoming more literate; newspapers making their appearance; and more cultured, providing concerts, plays, libraries, especially as Professor Wood commented for the fortunate minority.

☛ *See also Gawthern, Abigail*

GILL, GEORGE
The son of the curate and schoolmaster at Wilford, George Gill lived from 1778-1855. When he was twenty-one he set up his own business and later as a lace, thread and yarn agent, made a considerable fortune. He

This example of the style of Georgian architecture can be seen on High Pavement.

proceeded to use this in public benefactions. He gave £3,000 to start the People's College to give a higher education not available elsewhere, erected a Working Men's Retreat in Plantaganet Street and bought a former mansion in Heathcote Street. Intended for educational purposes, it later became a recreational and meeting place known as People's Hall. All three of these establishments still exist. A plaque commemorating George Gill's philanthropy was placed in People's Hall on Heathcote Street.

GREATER NOTTINGHAM

In his book *Nottingham Through 500 years* Duncan Gray entitled one chapter 'Greater Nottingham'. He was referring to Nottingham as it was after 1877, when the surrounding parishes became part of the borough. Later, influenced perhaps by the examples of Birmingham and Manchester, Nottingham would have liked the City to be extended taking in rural parishes and small urban districts, which surrounded it, thus creating, in effect, an even Greater Nottingham. However, the City Council received a bitter blow when the Government refused to grant its request in 1920.

A similar attempt ten years later received only partial success by bringing in some rural areas where the City was already building council houses. A similar limited extension was granted in 1952 bringing Clifton and Wilford into the City.

In recent years the term 'Greater Nottingham' has acquired a new meaning. It does not refer to a change in the City's area and local authority status, but to a concept. It arises from the changes which have taken place in a number of aspects of modern life. For instance, the City's transport department already serves such areas as Beeston, West Bridgford, Arnold and Carlton, and to a more limited extent Southwell, Newark and Loughborough and villages between them and Nottingham. The opening of the new express transit system, the 'tram' now connects Nottingham and Hucknall and other routes are being considered. The greater use of the motor car for travel and the opportunity to live further away from the City means that policies affecting road management and the siting of industry and housing need to consider the impact over a wider area than local authority boundaries. The changing pattern of shopping, education, cultural sectors and entertainment similarly have aspects which needed to be considered in a wider context.

A Greater Nottingham Partnership has been set up to encourage proper regard to this important concept.

GUARDIANS, NOTTINGHAM BOARD OF

Under the Statute of Elizabeth 1601 the responsibility of looking after those who could not maintain themselves – the poor, unemployed, aged, sick and children orphaned or abandoned – was placed on parishes. To meet the cost of poor relief they were empowered to raise money compulsorily by poor rates. These were based on the estimated value of a person's house, so that the rich with better houses paid more than those who lived in more modest ones.

The parishes could also build poor houses, or workhouses where they could provide raw materials, such as wool and cotton, so that inmates could make goods, which could be sold to reduce the cost to the ratepayers.

The system worked reasonably well in the seventeenth and early eighteenth centuries, in a mainly rural England, although with thousands of small parishes there were bound to be differences due to the parish inhabitants' attitudes. In Nottingham, each of the three parishes, St Mary, St Peter and St Nicholas, erected poor houses. By the beginning of the nineteenth century, the increased population in towns, the growing industrialisation and fluctuating economic conditions were putting increasing strain on the Old Poor Law as it became referred to later.

The system became increasingly the subject of politics and reform, with a Government inquiry. This resulted in the Poor Law Amendment Act 1834,

Arthur Marshall, architect

The laying of the foundation stone of Bagthorpe workhouse is commemorated by this plaque, which gives the names of the Guardians and of the architect Arthur Marshall (ARIBA).

which divided the country up into new administrative areas known as Unions, covering a number of parishes. Nottingham had its Board of Guardians elected in 1835 and its first few years were controversial. This was because the Poor Law Board, an arm of the Government took a keen interest in the Board's attempts to build a new workhouse in place of the three old ones. This was to lead to acrimony, as the workhouses were regarded by many as heartless prisons, 'Bastilles' being a common term. The workhouse was eventually built on a site between York Street and Huntingdon Street. The Guardians work consisted of paying money as relief to those in need, in the absence of any other provision apart from charity. To try and stop what it regarded as fecklessness, the Board could refuse this outdoor relief to the able bodied by offering them accommodation in the workhouse. This could not easily be enforced at times of unemployment, especially in Nottingham where there were few opportunities for alternative work when the textile trades were subject to changes in fashion and faced competition from abroad.

In the 1890s the workhouse site was taken for the construction of the new railway line and Victoria Station. The workhouse was demolished and a new one, with an infirmary, built at Bagthorpe (Hucknall Road). The Poor Laws came under increasing criticism in the twentieth century and Boards of Guardians were abolished in 1929. Their duties were taken over by the City Council under a Public Assistance Committee, its name being later altered to Social Welfare.

As part of the post-1946 political changes a National Assistance Act 1948 completely abolished the Poor Laws and the work transferred to national bodies as regards outdoor relief. Workhouses were done away with, the City Council forming a Welfare Services Committee for the elderly who could not care for themselves or be looked after by relatives. The care of children who were orphaned or abandoned or otherwise deprived of a normal life was transferred by the Children Act 1948 to a Children Committee.

GUILDHALL

In a charter of 1189, King Henry II granted Nottingham the right to have a Merchants' Guild, that is, a body which could represent the merchants of the borough and which was in effect an embryonic council or corporation. The place where the Guild had its meeting was the Guild Hall. The first written reference occurred in 1395. It was in Weekday Cross, which became the administrative centre of the English Borough. In 1478, a new Hall was built, a document giving the names of the supervisors of the work being printed in volume two of the Borough Records. It was used as a court as well as for the corporation, which had succeeded the guild. It was apparently used a lot as in 1581 when the chamberlains had to pay a penny 'for iyne per (juniper) to sweeten the Hall'.

It became known as the Guildhall in 1734 and the Council decided to build a new Hall in the market place, which when built was referred to as the Exchange, after originally being called the New Guildhall. The old one thereafter became the Town Hall. An engraving of the Hall and the Prison was made by Thomas Sandby in 1741 and a later one, in 1791, shows a completely different appearance after rebuilding. It continued to be used as the council's headquarters after the reformed council was elected in 1835 until 1888 when a new Guildhall was erected on Burton Street. It had a Grand Jury Room on the first floor, two magistrates' courts on the ground floor, but known as police courts numbers one and two, committee rooms, offices for staff and cells for prisoners.

It became in time the building in which the Town Clerks', Magistrates', City Engineers and Estates Departments' offices were situated. Later, extensions were added as far as North Church Street. The number of courts rose so much that additional ones were held in Sandfield House on Peachey Street.

The opening of the new Magistrates' Courts at the side of the Nottingham Canal resulted in the Guildhall becoming used as council offices only.

HEALTH AND SANITATION

The population of Nottingham increased in the last thirty years of the eighteenth century from about 10,000 to nearly 30,000. To house the increase, thousands of new houses were built. Because of the restriction of building on the common lands, the houses were built on any available plots, using up former gardens and orchards. There was no control of the quality of construction, no inspection of them to see if they were fit to live in and no planning of new streets, drains and sanitary matters. This state of affairs was to continue for over thirty-years into the nineteenth century until there was no land available for further development.

Many of the houses were built back-to-back and in courts with a tunnel entrance and houses facing each other across an open drain. Sewage and domestic refuse was allowed to accumulate until it was sold to contractors who carried it away by the canal into adjoining rural areas. In such conditions it was not surprising that diseases such as fever, diarrhoea, dysentery and tuberculosis were prevalent. The old corporation in 1802 were aware of the necessity to do something about this and when an end to the war was announced the corporation decided that instead of an illumination it would use the money, £10, to set up a fund. This was to help the sick poor or to erect a fever house 'an institution much wanted in the town'. In 1809 the jubilee of the King's accession was celebrated in Nottingham by the corporation subscribing one hundred guineas, some of which was to be allocated to the fund for the erection of a fever house whenever the foundation stone should be laid.

More positive action was required in 1832 when an outbreak of cholera occurred. This was a highly contagious disease, which could cause death within hours. Nine-hundred people caught the disease of whom 300 died. A Board of Health was set up which organised a temporary cholera hospital and a dispensary.

Despite this, little was done to improve living conditions in the poorer districts and to eradicate sources of diseases, even after the new corporation was set up, until national enquiries were held.

☞ *See also Health of Towns Commission*

HEALTH OF TOWNS COMMISSION

The 1830s in England was a time of reform – of Parliament, of the Poor Law and of Municipal Corporations. These were followed by many government inquiries on further matters, which called for information leading to further reforms. One of these was the Health of Towns Commission, under which an inspector visited Nottingham and submitted a report on his findings. The Inspector, J R Martin, wrote:

> *I believe that nowhere shall we find so large a mass of inhabitants crowded into courts, alleys and lanes as in Nottingham, cluttered yard within yard in a manner to defy description.*

He went on to describe the lack of sanitation, hygiene and squalor to be found in these courts and alleys.

These referred only to some parts of the borough. The differences between the poorest and worst parts compared to the better parts can be judged by the death rates of different wards. In Byron Ward the death rate was 30.9 per thousand people, whilst in Park Ward it was only 19.5.

Nottingham was not unique in this respect and as a result of the government inquiries, it passed a Nuisances Removal Act in 1846. 'Nuisance' had a far more condemnatory meaning than it has now. The council set up a committee to serve what needed to be done to comply with the Act. The survey revealed a number of matters of which they were apparently unaware. These included streets unpaved and undrained, others without sewers, collections of manure in open pits, plus pigstyes and bone boilers adjoining dwellings.

To try to remedy these conditions the Council appointed a Sanitary Committee. It continued to operate until 1871 and issued annual reports on what had been done. The committee had no powers of coercion and little public money to pay for improvements. It was handicapped by the fact that responsibility for conditions was shared to some extent with the Highway Boards, and the Board of Guardians and by the existence of the adjoining parishes through which the River Leen flowed. The latter was altered when the Borough Extension Act was passed in 1877.

Later in the nineteenth century, efforts were made to prevent many of the defects of the previous seventy years being perpetuated, notably when the council made it compulsory for all new buildings to be approved by the General Works and Highways Committee. The extent to which the situation in the older parts of the town was extended can be judged is found in the various clearance schemes of the twentieth century.

HEARTH TAX

Introduced in 1662 'for the better support of his Majesty's Crowne and dignity', the Hearth Tax was a fixed amount for each fire hearth in every house. The tax was collected in Nottingham by the petty constables or disnarys (decennaries) who had to submit lists showing the name of the occupiers and the number of the hearths. The lists for 1674 give the information under the names of the thirty-one decennaries and these have been published by the Thoroton Society, together with the lists for most of the county.

The list for the town contains 946 names, which equates to a total population of about 4,500 people. The households between them had 3,095 hearths, the number in each house varying from 1 to 9 in the majority of cases. There were another 21 houses which had 10 or more hearths, the largest number being in the Earl of Clare's house which had 47. This was Clare House, which had been built in the sixteenth century by Thomas Thurland. The next largest numbers were 23, Robert Pierrepont's house and 16 for Mr Malyn's; Mr Henry Plumtree's house had 14 hearths.

HORSE RACING

Although the racing of horses was known in England in Roman times and the Middle Ages, it was in the seventeenth century that it became known as the 'Sport of Kings'. This was due to the royal patronage it received and also to the selective breeding of thoroughbred horses. Nottingham had its racecourse on the land on its northern boundary called The Forest. In 1777 a large grandstand was built there, designed by a well-known architect, John Carr of York. The racing became a fashionable part of the social scene. In July 1776, Abigail Gawthern recorded in her diary that there was a large meeting, visited by the Duke and Duchess of Portland, Lord and Lady Lincoln, Lord and Lady Villers and a great many of the nobility.

Writing in 1853, William Wylie in *Old and New Nottingham* commented that the racecourse had declined from the grandeur of the previous century. Under the Municipal Reform Act 1835 the new council appointed a Race Committee to administer the racecourse and this was re-appointed each year

The Grosvenor Hotel *on Mansfield Road was conveniently close to Nottingham's racecourse for the landlord John H Williamson to ride in events there. His son, also called John, did even better, winning the Grand National once.*

until 1889, when racing on the Forest ceased. A new racecourse was then opened at Colwick, which is still functioning.

HOSIERY

In the medieval period, women would often augment the family income by knitting by hand, stockings, which in the days before men wore long trousers were in great demand. The Reverend William Lee, the vicar of Calverton in the Tudor period was engaged to be married to a young lady. She was one of those who knitted stockings by hand. This meant the Reverend Lee had to take second place to the knitting, so he invented a stocking-frame with an ingenious arrangement, which could make several pairs of stockings at once, thus giving the future Mrs Lee more time to devote to William.

Queen Elizabeth banned the use of these frames, which she thought would lead to unemployment. After a period in France, the stocking-frame came back to England in the seventeenth century. A cottage-based industry started to expand in villages in the East Midlands, especially in north-west Leicestershire, parts of Derbyshire and in southern and western Nottinghamshire. They were quite substantial machines, which required a certain amount of physical power to operate them. Men with capital purchased the frames, which were rented out to villagers and the men could operate in their own time, such as when it was not possible to work on the land. The women and children could also help in such things as winding the yarn and filling the shuttles. The hosiers who rented out the frames would supply the yarn, cotton, wool or silk and collect the finished goods, paying them for their time. The hosiers would then arrange for the goods to be packaged and distributed to retailers.

As Nottingham became more industrialised in the late eighteenth century, some of the better-off inhabitants with large houses moved out of the town to more rural parts. The hosiers would buy their houses and live in them and use them for storage. Many of them found it convenient to live near each other, which was helpful to their trade.

By the beginning of the nineteenth century Nottingham hosiery became increasingly unprofitable because the northern factories and mills, powered by fast flowing streams and by steam could make goods cheaper. The stockingers including some who lived in or near Nottingham were entirely dependent on the trade to earn a living and were reduced to having to accept very low wages. This caused considerable unrest and agitation.

Nottingham was fortunate in that lace became the staple industry later in the century, but hosiery survived when steam-powered machines were developed and the two industries between them employed thousands especially women. The stocking-frames survived in a few special sections, one branch making Shetland-type shawls.

In the twentieth century the demand for lace fell and the industry declined. Hosiery continued to flourish for a time until it was unable to compete with countries in the Far East, with much lower wages. The number of factories is still declining in Nottingham.

☛ **See also Luddism**

This engraving of the stocking frame, which revolutionised the hosiery industry, was reproduced in Deering's *History of Nottingham.*

THE STOCKING FRAME

T. Sandby Del   J. Close Sc

HOSPITALS

The first hospital, in the modern sense, was the General Hospital erected by public subscription in 1781 on a site just outside the borough. It remained a voluntary hospital until 1948, when it became part of the National Health Service. An elegant nurses' home was erected as a memorial to the First World War and a large multi-storey ward was built in the 1960s. The building of a new teaching hospital, the Queen's Medical Centre, on Derby Road, Lenton, resulted in the closure of the General Hospital. Some of the buildings, including the Jubilee Tower, the chapel and offices have been retained and used for other purposes. The 1960s block was demolished but the nurses' home has been converted

The General Hospital no longer exists but some of its buildings are used for other purposes. The plaque is still in place on Park Row.

Mapperley Hospital for the mentally ill occupied a large part of Porchester Road. The remaining buildings are here seen from Ransom Road with newer buildings erected on sites of other parts.

into flats. Other buildings have been erected on the site, including offices and living accommodation.

A children's hospital was opened in Chestnut Grove, off Mapperley Road, and a new Women's Hospital was built on Peel Street in 1931, replacing earlier adapted buildings. The work for both these has been absorbed elsewhere, since the Queen's Medical Centre was opened. Both buildings have been retained, the former Women's Hospital being converted to flats.

Since the early seventeenth century, hospital accommodation for the elderly and the poor had been provided in various ways by parishes. In Nottingham, St Mary's parish workhouse and infirmary were replaced, after much controversy, by the Board of Guardians, on York Street. When the Great Central Railway and Victoria Station came to Nottingham, the workhouse was demolished and a new one built at Sherwood. The workhouse function ceased in 1948 and the infirmary, renamed the City Hospital was administered by the City Council until 1948, when it became part of the National Health Service. It has been modernised and greatly expanded since, a process still continuing.

HOUSING COMMITTEE, 1909 TO 1919

On 11 January 1909 the first City Council committee to deal specifically with housing problems met. It appointed Councillor Milner, a doctor of medicine, as chairman. This was something of a personal triumph for him, for he had tried on eight or nine times to persuade the Council to appoint such a committee.

This decision was the outcome of a survey, which had been carried out by council members since 1907 into the conditions in some of the worst parts of the city and to decide what could be done to deal with them. At the same time the government was passing a Bill through Parliament in an attempt to do the same throughout the country. Nottingham therefore waited until the Bill became law, which it did as the Housing and Town Planning Act 1909.

It was not that there was any lack of statutory powers affecting housing, as in the last quarter of the nineteenth century three such Acts had been passed, with little success mainly due to inertia of Local Authorities. All three Acts were named as applying to artisans, labourers or the working classes, as the rest of society was deemed able to fend for themselves. There has also been a Royal Commission, which did not achieve a great deal. Part of the lack of progress was the widely felt antipathy to spending public money. Nottingham's Health Committee and the Medical Officer had earlier shown such opposition and it was Councillor Milner's campaign that resulted in the power to deal with housing being transferred from the Health Committee to the Housing Committee.

The Committee at once set about inspecting some of the worst properties in Radford and then carried out a policy of co-operating with some of the property owners. This involved them in closing some unfit houses, or using them for other than housing. Other methods included giving some compensation for carrying out improvements, which reduced their incomes. The Committee submitted annual reports to the Council, including photographs showing examples of what had been done.

Their main task, however, was to press for large-scale clearance of areas such as Red Lion Street (Narrow Marsh) and to oversee its subsequent redevelopment. This had to be postponed because of the cost, but it was later carried out just after the end of the 1914–18 war. Another scheme was similar, the Carter Gate Clearance Area. This did go ahead and by 1914, some £60,000 had been spent on acquiring and demolishing houses in an area which was later used for the creation of the Wholesale Market at Sneinton and the City Transport offices and Depot on Southwell Road. This scheme too had to be postponed until after the war.

Under the Housing Act of 1919, the Housing Committee received additional powers, which for the next sixty years helped it to build over 60,000 new dwellings and to carry out extensive clearance and redevelopment of older houses.
☛ *See also Council Houses*

HUDSON, KITTY
Born at Arnold on 9 March 1765, Kitty Hudson came to live in Nottingham when she was six years of age. At that time fashionable ladies used pins and needles in various ways in keeping their finery in order. Some of these apparently found their way to church floors. Kitty was employed when still quite young in sweeping a Nottingham church two or three times a week. Another girl a few years older than Kitty asked her to collect any such items for which she was rewarded with a toffee. Whenever Kitty found these sought after items, she was in the habit of holding them in her mouth until she had finished work. Inevitably some of these were swallowed from time to time and this unusual diet soon had repercussions, causing sleeplessness and loss of appetite. She was admitted to Nottingham General Hospital in August 1783 where a Dr Hugh Moises treated her over many months by removing pins and needles by various surgical means. He later wrote a detailed account of her treatment.

After she was discharged she married and had nineteen children.

HUTCHINSON, COLONEL JOHN
John Hutchinson was born at Nottingham in 1616, the son of Sir Thomas Hutchinson. After he married in 1638 he settled at Owthorpe, a small village near Bingham. When the Civil War broke out he decided to support the

Parliamentary side. In 1643 he was appointed Governor of the Town with headquarters in the Castle. Numerous skirmishes took place and on one occasion the Royal troops fired on the Castle from the tower of St Nicholas church. Colonel Hutchinson ordered the church to be demolished to prevent further such use and in 1651 also ordered the demolition of the Castle. After the restoration of the monarchy in 1660, as he had been one of the signatories to the King's death warrant, he was imprisoned in Sandown Castle, where he died in 1664.

Colonal Hutchinson's widow, Lucy, after his death wrote his biography which has been reprinted many times.

INFANT MORTALITY

For centuries, people in England had been aware of the fact that when a child was born its chances of survival beyond the age of five were doubtful. When the expected span of life was much lower than it is today, this too seemed to be part of life. When industry started to be more productive because of steam power, the population of England started to increase. Why it did is still a matter of some conjecture, but statistically it was due to people living longer, as demonstrated by the excess of births over deaths.

In 1837 the national registration of births, marriages and deaths was introduced and was compulsory. The nineteenth century had witnessed a growing concern amongst a small minority of professional men, reformers and medical men, about social evils and inequalities. They also had a passion for recording and publishing statistics of all kinds to prove their points.

There were men such as these in Nottingham including some on the Borough Council. In March 1852, the Sanitary Committee gave the council figures, which the General Board of Health had produced for Nottingham.

The reality of infant mortality is brought home by this tombstone in the Church Cemetery.

These included the number of deaths in the town in the seven years from 1844 to 1850. These totalled 10,163, an average of 1,490 a year, with some wide variations in particular years. In 1847 the highest number was 1,684, and in 1850 the lowest 1,290. The Sanitary Committee itself calculated the number of deaths in the same period of children under five. These amounted to 4,526, 44 per cent of all deaths.

The Committee later in the year published figures of deaths in the three months of July, August and September. The total was 409 and of these 196 were children under five, whilst for those under one year accounted for the vast majority of 150. Moreover, the Committee produced the figures for each of the seven wards of the town. Two of the seven wards, Byron and St Ann's, each had almost twice as many inhabitants each as the other wards, forming 40 per cent of the population. The deaths in Byron and St Ann's Wards were equal to 36 per 1,000 people, whilst in Sherwood and Park Wards the number was only 14 per 1,000.

These figures clearly indicated the wide gulf between the worst living conditions in the low lying parts of the town, with its crowded slums and little sanitation, and the newer parts on higher ground with natural drainage. To iron out these differences would take many years of demolishing the older houses and building new ones. This took another 130 years to carry out but this was not the only remedy needed. Figures published in 2004 have showed that the expectation of life in different parts of the City show marked differences still.

Today, these differences can be attributed to differences in incomes, diets and education. In 1852, these differences were magnified by the conditions then existing. They were so great, particularly in respect of lack of education and knowledge of childcare that whilst progress was made in other directions throughout the nineteenth century, infant mortality remained stubbornly high. In 1895 it was 189 out of every 1,000 births, a third of all deaths. This was to decrease steadily for the first quarter of the twentieth century when it fell, in Nottingham, to around 90, although this was still higher than the figure for England and Wales. After a short period of levelling out, the rate fell continually to about 15, today's figure for both Nottingham and England and Wales.

This reduction was achieved by the better medical care, including midwifery and by the greater recognition of the value of maternity and child welfare services.

INFECTIOUS DISEASES – NOTIFICATION

In 1871–72 an outbreak of smallpox in Nottingham resulted in 99 deaths. The following year the town's first Medical Officer of Health was appointed. Such an appointment had been considered in 1859 but the council did not approve. Under the Public Health Act 1872 the town was required to make such an appointment and Dr Edward Seaton became the first. It was no doubt his recommendation that resulted in the town obtaining a local Act in 1878, in which power was given to make compulsory the notification of infectious diseases. The Health Committee ruled that this be applied to smallpox and scarlet fever, for a period not exceeding a year. This provoked a protest from thirty-eight of the town's medical practitioners. Their reasons included that information received from patients should be as 'secret as those of the confessional'. Other reasons were given such as that mortality in hospitals was greater than for persons treated at home and that patients were likely to catch diseases in hospitals worse than the ones for which they were admitted.

In a long report submitted to the council by the Health Committee, Dr Seaton strongly defended the proposal and rebutted the doctors' objections.

In 1891 the Council resolved to adopt the provisions of the Infectious Diseases (Prevention) Act, which were not compulsory. These included inspection of dairies, cleaning of infected bedding and clothing and the detention in hospitals of infected persons who had no proper lodging.

JEWS
The earliest records of Jews in England occur after the Norman invasion of England following massacres in France and the Rhineland in 1096. Very few seemed to have come to Nottingham although the names of three were recorded in 1193–4. There were more of them in the thirteenth century as recorded in taxation records. These show that they were not as wealthy or numerous as were Jews in York and Lincoln. A synagogue is mentioned in a deed dated 1257.

Because of their financial acumen Jews were tolerated by the monarchs until 1290 when a Decree of Expulsion meant most of them left the country. This was because of other financiers from Europe and of increasing hostility from the church, barons and gentry. However, not all left England and some remained in Nottingham. In 1467–8 a court record refers to Edwardus Judaeus who changed his name to George Lambert. There are other brief references to Jews in Nottingham up to the end of the eighteenth century but it is not until the beginning of the nineteenth century that a Jewish community became established. Most of the early members were engaged in the burgeoning textile trades in Nottingham and some came from Germany with a two-way trade between the two countries. By 1822 there were sufficient for them to acquire land on North Sherwood Street for a burial ground. This small plot is still there hidden behind a wall but is not used as such now.

The 1830s and 1840s saw an increasing number of Jews coming to Nottingham not only as textile tradesmen but also of professional men. Not all continued in the Jewish faith, and some were converting to other faiths.

About 1835 Lewis Heymann married and came to live in Nottingham where he became a member of the High Pavement Unitarian Chapel. He was already a successful businessman in a partnership, Heymann and Alexander. He was able to take West Bridgford Hall on lease, become an Alderman on the Town Council and Mayor of Nottingham.

An important step for the community was the inauguration of the Chaucer Street Formal congregation, although it was not until 1890 that a synagogue was built there. In the interim period services were held in various, sometimes unsatisfactory, premises such as rooms above a factory. The President of the new church was Mr Albert Cahn who came to England from Germany as a young man and established a furniture business. His son, Julian, became the owner of the business in due course. He was noted for his charitable benefactions, presenting Newstead Abbey to Nottingham Corporation as well as other donations. He became a baronet, living at Stanford Hall and was well known for his private cricket team for which he secured the services of some fine cricketers.

The story of Jews in Nottingham in the twentieth century includes the purchase of the former Methodist church building on Shakespeare Street as a Synagogue and the Progressive Jewish Congregation Synagogue at Sherwood. These and other events, as well as the record of the contribution by Jews, both men and women are contained in the book *Eight Hundred Years – The Story of Nottingham's Jews* by Nelson Fisher, published in 1998.

LACE

The making of lace has been carried out for centuries by hand, a process known as bobbin net or cushion lace. This involved using threads to form hexagonal shapes in the form of a mesh. When the stocking frame was invented it was able to make knitted goods much quicker than could be done by hand. This led Nottingham's mechanically minded smiths to consider how the same principle could be applied to making lace by a similar machine. At first the efforts were limited to making a basic knitted mesh and adding decorative features. This was not wholly satisfactory as the basic knitted squares suffered from the disadvantage that cutting one square caused a whole row to collapse. The hexagonal lace structure did not suffer in this way if cut. John Heathcoat, a framesmith who completed his apprenticeship in 1804, came to Nottingham. Here, a few years later, he perfected a machine, which successfully made lace by a method of producing a hexagonal mesh. This was sufficiently different from the stocking frame for Heathcoat to patent his bobbin net or twist net machine. Although he licensed some people to make and operate such machines it was not until his patent expired in 1823 that several ingenious Nottingham mechanics were able to make similar machines and to improve them.

One of these was the use of punched cards, known as jacquards, to create different patterns. The 1820s saw the emergence of what became known as the twist-net fever. Many men who were able to afford to buy or rent a machine did so, often operating them in their own homes or small workshops. New suburbs such as New Basford and Carrington were started to house the growing number of such men. It was however one thing to make lace, but to sell it and make a profit was another. Lace was subject to fashion and this together with over production caused failures of businesses.

Fortunately, a combination of entrepreneurial skill and steam-power enabled a factory lace industry to be established by 1850. The subsequent development is described below under the heading Lace Market.

LACE MARKET

The structure of the lace industry followed that of the hosiery industry. Both needed various stages of production, which could be carried out by different operatives and when the product was finished the commercial operations – finishing, storage, distribution, accounting – had to be carried out by other specialists. Both industries were capital intensive and so needed entrepreneurs with access to finance.

1 Weekday Cross still has 'W Cotton' in stone over the door, but curtains at 1/- (one shilling) per pair are no longer sold there.

For the hosiery industry, the stages after the initial production were carried out by a new breed of capitalists, master hosiers. The manufacture on stocking frames was not carried out entirely in the borough, but was widespread throughout the East Midlands. The hosiers found it convenient to have their residences, often combined with their businesses in Nottingham. The town, in the eighteenth century was still confined to its medieval boundaries but in the early years there was still room for building new houses for the gentry who could afford them. The later industrialisation and increase of population caused the gentry to move to more salubrious rural areas outside the town. The master hosiers took the opportunity to move into the vacant houses in which they could live and carry on their businesses.

A similar situation arose in the early nineteenth century when lace manufacture started to outstrip hosiery. The equivalent to master hosiers, the

One can now see and buy lace at Numbers 3 and 5 High Pavement.

lace manufacturers (who despite their description did not actually make lace – this was done by lace makers) tended to congregate in the Castle Gate/Hounds Gate area. The growth of the lace industry both in quantity and complexity influenced two lace manufacturers in particular, Thomas Adams and Richard Birkin, to have new architect designed purpose built lace warehouses built. Both these were in Stoney Street and designed by architect Thomas Chambers Hine. Birkin had acquired an eighteenth century mansion, Plumtre House, on land adjoining St Mary's Church. He had the house demolished and built his warehouses on a new street, Broadway, connecting St Mary's Gate and Stoney Street. Thomas Adams' warehouse, built in the E-shape of a medieval mansion incorporated features not hitherto regarded as necessary in an industrial building. An enlightened Anglican, he provided rest rooms for employees, heating and a chapel with a paid clergyman who conducted a short service for employees each morning.

These two buildings set the standard for the construction of other warehouses in the area, which became known as the Lace Market. The site was practically coterminous with the Anglo-Saxon borough and the medieval street pattern was mainly retained.

The term Lace Market did not relate to a retail market but was used in the sense of a centre for a common purpose, such as the Stock Market. The warehouses were not merely places for storage but housed workplaces for lace finishing processes such as singeing, repairing and embroidery. They also had the offices for selling finished products, invoicing and accounting. The grandeur of some of the larger warehouses was intended to impress visitors with the quality of the lace products including the Victorian symbol of respectability, lace curtains. The second half of the nineteenth century saw lace become the staple trade of Nottingham, with a national and international market.

By 1900 the re-building of the Lace Market had become virtually completed. It had resulted in the disappearance of some hundreds of old dwelling houses and some gardens and orchards, but retained St Mary's church, a Wesleyan chapel, the Shire Hall, the old Town Hall, a theatre and some of the gentry houses.

The period from 1900 to 1914 saw the English lace trade facing increasing competition from European countries, as well as the ever present changes of fashion. The outbreak of War in 1914, with the loss of the export trade dealt the blow from which it never fully recovered. A brief revival in the 1920s saw further changes in fashion and methods of production. Many of the buildings became occupied by other trades, sometimes leading to multi-occupation. Although the Second World War created a demand for products which the lace industry could supply, such as camouflage nets, it did not help the Lace Market itself. War time restrictions meant that maintenance of the buildings suffered.

The run down nature of the area, with its shabby soot-blackened buildings raised the question of whether the Lace Market should be re-developed with demolition of at least some of the buildings. Fortunately, the passing of the Civic Amenities Act of 1968 gave the City Council the opportunity to create the Lace Market a conservation area. The City Council helped to rejuvenate the area, by financial means in some cases, including cleaning of soot-blackened buildings and by encouragement of proper re-development. This included setting up a Lace Market Development Company.

The Company in conjunction with the City Council has in the last few years done much to transform the Lace Market. Some of the former warehouses have been converted to other uses, such as bars, clubs and also apartments. Some new apartments have also been built. A major success has been the transformation of the former Adams building into New College Nottingham. Recently much of the older property in the area between Fletcher Gate and St Mary's Gate has been demolished and new buildings erected for apartments and leisure facilities.

LEEN VALLEY

The little River Leen, which gives its name to the valley rises about five miles north of the City border at Bulwell. From there it flows in almost a circle until it enters the River Trent. It provided suitable sites for the four Anglo-Saxon settlements of Bulwell, Basford, Radford and Lenton, before flowing through the borough on its way to the Trent. Its natural resources were supplemented for industrial use, by providing water for mills. With the

This old mill photograph shows how water was taken from the river and used to power a water wheel to drive machinery.

growth of the textile trades from the seventeenth century, it also became a source of supply for bleaching, dyeing and for conversion to steam. The increasing population from the late eighteenth century resulted in the river becoming an open sewer. Because of its connection with the borough, the Council became increasingly concerned about the threat to health and in 1872 it set up, in conjunction with the adjoining parishes, the Nottingham, and Leen District Sewerage Board. Little progress was made in improving the situation, because of the divided loyalties of the five constituent areas. This led, amongst other aspects, to the extension of the borough in 1877.

With only one controlling authority, it resulted in some improvement in drainage and sewerage, although it was to be many years before industrial pollution of the river was ended.

Flooding of the former parishes continued to be a problem throughout the twentieth century from time to time, but remedial works seemed to have solved that problem. Because of the gradient-free course of the river, the valley also provided the route for a railway line.

LENTON

In Domesday Book, Lenton appears to have been very much like the other vills along the River Leen, although the King had four bovates of land there.

The original premises of the Lenton Co-operative Society are on Church Street/Radford Boulevard. The Society was absorbed in the Nottingham Co-operative Society.

It was, however, to become much different in the twelfth century when a Cluniac priory was established there by William Peverel, the constable of Nottingham Castle. It grew to be the wealthiest of the monasteries in the county and became the owner of lands from which it drew income. It was also granted its own fair, which rivalled Nottingham's and was a source of friction at times. It was, however, one of the earliest victims of Henry VIII's dissolution. After the dissolution much of the land became the property of two Nottingham families, the Gregorys and the Sherwins.

In the eighteenth century a turnpike road from Nottingham to Derby and later the Nottingham Canal passed through the parish. It was a large parish and had several large houses in the southern part. At the 1801 census its population had risen to 893, but started to grow more rapidly. By 1832 the population was 3,077 and Lenton, like the adjoining borough and other parishes, had become industrialised largely due to the textile trade. Lenton had new parts nearer to Nottingham known as New Lenton. It became part of the borough in 1877 and one result of this was the construction of the boulevards, which became part of an inner ring road.

Lenton continued to expand with other industries including a large leather works and later the Raleigh Cycle Company's offices and works. It has seen many changes in the twentieth century starting with the new premises for what is now the University of Nottingham. A new Jubilee Campus was added to the University in 1997. Another important addition is the Queen's Medical Centre. The pharmaceutical empire of Boots built new premises on the border with Beeston, the complex being partly in each of the two areas. Another far-reaching new development was the industrial estate either side of the re-routed A52 from Clifton Bridge.

LEVERS, JOHN

Born at Sutton-in-Ashfield in 1786, John Levers came to live at Radford in about 1813. He is said to have spent two years more or less as a recluse experimenting with making improvements to existing machines for making point net and warp lace. His efforts were so successful that a branch of the lace trade became known as the Levers branch. He died in France in 1848.

This Holbrook bequest plaque can be seen on a wall near Canning Circus near to the site of the house where he lived. His surname was properly 'Levers'

LIBRARIES

The early nineteenth century in Nottingham was marked by the foundation of libraries. Reference is made earlier to the Bromley House Subscription Library formed in 1817, but was restricted to the wealthier and more educated class. There was also a demand for facilities to be made available for those of the working class to satisfy the growing desire to be better educated. A number of operatives' libraries were housed in public houses where members could meet. An Artisans Library started in 1824 and met a need for about forty years, until free libraries were established in 1867. The Mechanics' Institute founded in 1837 also had a library, which continued until 1968 when the former building was replaced by a new one.

In 1855 the government passed a Public Libraries Act, which

In 1974, Nottinghamshire County Council became the library authority for the whole county including the City. It acquired Henry Barker's furniture shop and converted it to the Central Library.

towns could adopt if they so wished. This was accompanied by power to levy a small rate for the purpose. When it was suggested in 1867 that Nottingham should have a library, a survey found that twenty-six towns had already adopted the Act. The Council thereupon appointed a Free (Public) Library and Museum Committee. It opened the first library in 1868 in premises on Thurland Street. By 1876 it had 2,093 registered readers.

In 1881 the University College on Shakespeare Street was opened. The part of the premises at the junction of Sherwood Street and Shakespeare Street became a Free Library. By the end of the century the number of readers was about 10,000. A reading room in Pine Street Chapel, Radford, was opened in 1892, as was Hyson Green Branch Library. A Reading Room was opened in 1900 on Carlton Road. A plan to build four district libraries in 1912, supported by a Carnegie Grant, had to be abandoned due to the outbreak of war in 1914.

The 1920s and 1930s saw the building of new branch libraries in places such as Basford and Sneinton, and others were built on new housing estates after the 1939–45 war.

In 1974 the City lost its status as a library authority to Nottinghamshire County Council. The latter converted a former furniture shop on Angel Row to a Central Library, replacing the Sherwood Street one. This included a Local Studies Library, which has accumulated a large illustrations collection.

In 1998 Nottingham regained its former status and resumed control of all the public libraries within the City. In recent years, the public libraries have extended their services by providing tapes and videos which can be borrowed and by installing micro-film and micro-fiche readers, as well as computers linked to the internet.

☛ *See also Mechanics' Institute*

LUDDISM

The term 'Luddite' has become a synonym for opposition to the replacement of manpower or traditional machinery by new forms. This dates back to the first decade of the nineteenth century when the stocking-frame industry in Nottingham and adjoining areas was starting to decline because of competition from the more advanced industrial north. This led to violent industrial action by aggrieved workers, known as 'Luddites', from a mythical leader called Ned Ludd.

Violence was nothing new in Nottingham as in 1779 when conditions in the stocking-frame industry were the subject of a petition to Parliament. When a Bill to improve conditions was rejected, riots in the town resulted in windows of hosiers being broken, the demolition of a house and furniture, and breaking of frames.

In March 1811 the first of the 'Luddite' frame breaking took place at Arnold, after a demonstration in Nottingham Market Place. Attacks were to take place sporadically until 1817. In that year a man named Diggle was hanged for having attempted to shoot a householder during a frame breaking. This seemed to end the 'Luddites'.

MARKETS

The importance of Nottingham's role as a trading centre and market was emphasised in the charter of King Henry II which stipulated that the men of Derbyshire and Nottinghamshire should come to the borough on Fridays and Saturdays with their wains and packhorses.

The growth of the two separate boroughs, the English and the French, meant that they should each have a separate place set aside for trading. The English borough used Weekday Cross for this purpose whilst the Norman borough had a market at the end of Friar Lane. Eventually the two markets merged to form what was to be for centuries the heart of Nottingham.

Deering in his book written in the 1740s has a long and graphic description of the scene:

This place has since the year 1711 received great additions. It was formerly divided lengthways in two by a wall breast high.

On the north side between the wall and Long Row was the Corn Market, with as well malt, oatmeal and salt. There were also many stalls for milliners, pedlars, sale-shops, hardware men, bakers, turners, brasiers, tinmen, chandlers and callar-makers. He goes on to describe the parts of the market occupied for different types of merchandise. At the Butter Cross sat those who sold butter, eggs and bacon, near to the Fruit Market with all kinds of fruits in season.

The Central Market turned into a Festival Market for one of the City's annual festivals in the 1960s.

As the population grew in the nineteenth century the buildings on Long Row, South Parade and Beastmarket Hill were either converted into shops or demolished and new purpose built ones erected. The market continued to be a popular venue, serving into the evening with naphtha lamps for illumination. After the enclosure of the Lammas Fields, Goose Fair lost its former site and moved into the Market Place. It had now become more of a pleasure fair, with amusements and stalls occupying the streets nearby.

All this was to change in the 1920s when it was decided to demolish the old Exchange and build a new Council House. To provide a fitting approach to the Council House, the market was moved to a Central Market, newly erected as a covered market. This was to be relatively short-lived as forty years later, when Victoria Station was demolished and Victoria Centre shopping mall built, space was allocated for market stalls.

MAYOR

The word 'mayor', derived from the same Latin word as 'major' was used quite early on in England, signifying a man who was the leading inhabitant of a borough and one who regulated trade and customs as well as justice. Nottingham was granted the right to appoint such a position in a charter of King Edward I in 1284. The burgesses were to appoint a mayor each year from among themselves. In return they were required to pay the royal exchequer a yearly sum of £60, an increase of £8 more than previously.

To celebrate the 700th anniversary of the Charter Mayor, in 1984, this photograph of the civic party was reproduced as a postcard invitation to an exhibition. The Lord Mayor was Councillor Mrs Ivy Matthews and the Sheriff Councillor Frank Dennett, with Mr Michael Hammond, Chief Executive.

King Henry VI also granted Nottingham a charter in 1449. This gave the borough freedom from the jurisdiction of the county by making Nottingham a county in itself, as well as a borough. It also granted the burgesses the right to appoint seven aldermen, one of whom was always to be Mayor. The aldermen were appointed for life unless they resigned the office or were removed for 'any notable cause'. This meant that the aldermen were the rulers of the town, although they later appointed senior and junior councillors to form a ruling body, though in fact the aldermen remained the virtual rulers. They retained this until 1835 when the old corporation as it became known was abolished by Act of Parliament. The same provided for councillors to be elected by burgesses and others who qualified for a vote as property owners. The councillors when elected chose a mayor, who could be anyone who was qualified to vote in elections. They could also elect seven aldermen who with the forty-two councillors became the new corporation. In practice, aldermen were almost always elected from the councillors. Aldermen were no longer elected for life, but for a six-year period, after which they could be, and usually were, re-elected.

The title of mayor was granted further distinction in 1928, when the Mayor became Lord Mayor. In 1974 a re-organisation of local government abolished the role of alderman, but the Lord Mayor continued to be appointed.

MEADOWS

Before the enclosure of the Meadows, one of the former common lands of the borough, they were famous for their springtime displays of crocuses. Fortunately two of Nottingham's foremost nineteenth century artists recorded in colour their charm.

That by Thomas Hammond was simply entitled *Crocuses* and was reproduced as the frontispiece of the book of his drawings published in 1926. The volume also included *The Last Dying Speech of the Crocuses*, a poem in eight verses by Anne Gilbert (1782 – 1866), the first of which is as follows:

> *Ye tender-hearted gentle folk of Nottingham's fair town and ye who have*
> *   loved us from the poet to the clown*
> *Attend our sore complainings, while with one accord we weep*
> *From mossy beds uprising, where sought over summer sleep.*

The painting by Samuel Oscroft was entitled *Crocus Gatherers* and it also showed the one existing building in the Meadows, the pinder's house. The gatherers too would have regretted the disappearance of the crocuses, a source of income.

From time to time, there have been suggestions that the crocuses were of the Autumnal flowering variety. However, in a speech delivered in 1901 by a

This painting shows the pre-enclosure meadows with its display of crocuses.

Mrs Anne Gilbert, which was reproduced in a book, she said:

The Meadows .....nothing but a vast stretch of beauteous meadow land – a lovely sight, especially in early spring when the purple crocuses in rich profession lent an annual charm.

The charm was intended to be maintained in a small way by naming one of the new Meadows streets, Crocus Street. In the post-war period, the Light Programme on the radio often had programmes, which played listeners' requests. On one of these the announcer enthused over an address, 'Crocus Street, the Meadows' as delightfully rural. Today's Crocus Street is hardly that but when the remark was made, it was decidedly less attractive with factories and terraces of houses either side of the street.

The Meadows became developed in the period 1860–1900 by factories, workshops, shops, public houses and in some parts by poor houses. These were demolished as a clearance area in the 1970s. The redevelopment restructured the Meadows by confining through traffic to the perimeters.

MECHANICS' INSTITUTE, NOTTINGHAM

The Industrial Revolution of the late eighteenth century, which substituted machine power for hand or muscle power in some industries, required a new class of worker, the mechanic, to make, maintain or operate machinery. The need to educate and instruct mechanics soon became apparent and Mechanics' Institutes were established in several towns. Nottingham mainly due to the efforts of a Nottingham banker, John Smith Wright and other

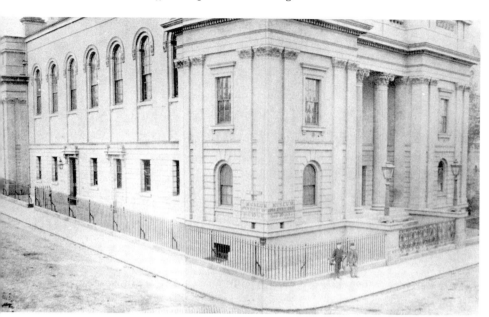

This shows the second Mechanics' Institute building, which was demolished in 1968.

interested men, founded a Nottingham Mechanics' Institute in 1837. This was not unanimously approved as some regarded them hot beds of sedition and irreligion, fostering a revolutionary spirit.

A meeting was held in the Town Hall, with the Mayor as chairman and it was agreed to form a Committee to organise the venture. The membership fee was set at a low rate of one shilling a quarter, but those who could afford more were encouraged to do so. Number 17 St James Street was acquired as the home of the institute and a library of 700 volumes had been acquired.

A librarian was appointed at a yearly salary of twelve guineas. A programme of lectures for 1839, twenty-eight in all, included subjects such as astronomy, physiology, botany, railways, as well as music and poetry.

In 1840 an exhibition was held in the Exchange to raise funds for the building of a new home for the Institute. This made a profit of £802, and a large new hall, the largest in the town, was opened in 1845. This building was burned down and a new one erected in 1869 on the same site. This remained, with an addition alongside, until 1968 when it was demolished and Birkbeck House erected on the site with shops on the ground floor, and offices in addition to the rooms for the Mechanics' Institute itself. This is empty at the time of writing and plans for the redevelopment of the site have been approved. Another new Mechanics' Institute has been built and is occupied, on North Sherwood Street.

The institute's early objective of imparting learning to those for whom there was no other provision was continued until other forms of formal education became available. The Institute continued to flourish with all kinds of popular but refined entertainment. It eventually became as well a centre for clubs and societies such as chess and photographic, gymnasium activities and rambling clubs. It also catered for indoor pastimes such as whist, billiards, snooker and cribbage, as part of a citywide network of competitive organisations. Despite its present appeal to artisans and mechanics being a thing of the past, it remains as a popular social centre.
☛ *See also Music Halls*

MICKLETORN JURY

In the years after the Normans came to England they introduced the manorial system of local administration of justice. The all-powerful Lord of the Manor had a Court Baron at which more serious offences were dealt with, whilst his subjects had a Court Leet for less serious crimes, disputes and nuisances. Nottingham had a Mickletorn, derived from the Latin for 'great court'. When Nottingham had a mayor and borough status the Mickletorn became the Borough Court. The former Mickletorn had a jury, which continued to flourish. Its role was to act as a watchdog on behalf of the burgesses. It used to inspect the borough from time to time and report any transgressions to the Court, which could take appropriate action.

One of the earliest records of the proceedings of the Jury is a list of their presentments or accusations. These numbered fifty-nine and many of them were directed at the various types of traders for alleged unfair dealing. 'All the female poulterers sell garlic, flour, salt, tallow, candles, butter, cheeses and such things too dearly'. Each of them were also said to make candles without wicks to the deception of the people. Similar complaints were made against the brewers, bakers, butchers, fishers, taverners of wine, tanners, shoemakers, cooks, hotel keepers, weavers, fullers and dyers. It seems as though the whole of the tradesmen of the town were corrupt. Unfortunately there is no record of what happened to them.

The other presentments were against named individuals for throwing ordure into the streets, or erecting tenements on common lands. The jury also used to 'beat the bounds' by inspecting the town boundaries to check any infringements. For this they were provided with a dinner. In 1869, they were still perambulating but only once in seven years. On that occasion the jurors complained that they could not proceed as usual as the railway was in their way. The jury expired peacefully on 21 October 1880.

MORLEY, SAMUEL

The letter 'I' in the name of the Nottingham hosiery firm of I and R Morley stood for John, 'I' and 'J' being interchangeable. John had a son, Samuel, in 1809

The bust of Samuel Morley is just inside the main entrance to the Arboretum. The inscription reads: Member of Parliament Merchant and Philanthropist Friend of Children Social Reformer Christian Citizen.

who became the sole managing partner of the firm with its headquarters in London. He became active in public affairs and was elected as MP for Nottingham in 1865 but was unseated due to the questionable electioneering of some of his supporters. He later became MP for Bristol for seventeen years. He was noted for his many charitable and philanthropic interests. He gave £500 to Nottingham Council to establish a children's library. He died in 1886 and a full length statue of him was erected outside the Theatre Royal. His bust in the Arboretum gives details of his qualities but does not record that when the statue had to be moved in 1929 it fell off the back of a lorry, and now only the head remains.

MUNDELLA, ANTHONY JOHN

Anthony Mundella was born in Leicester in 1823 but came to Nottingham, where at the age of twenty-three, he was made a partner in a hosiery firm, Hine and Mundella. The firm built one of the first large factories in Nottingham and Mundella became a member of the Town Council after he had been appointed Sheriff in 1853. He was elected as MP for Sheffield and served for twenty-nine years. He became Minister for Education and later President of the Board of Trade. He died in 1897.

MUSIC HALLS

The increasing population of Nottingham from the end of the eighteenth century was accompanied by an increased number of public houses. *Pigot's Directory* of 1828–29 listed under 'Nottingham' 250 taverns and public houses, but 50 of these were outside the borough at places such as Basford, Bulwell, Hyson Green and Arnold. The remaining 200 were all situated within a radius of 500 yards around the Market Place. For a population of 50,000, this represented one public house for every 60 or so adult men. Women generally did not frequent such places. With few other attractions for the working classes, public houses with no control of the hours they were open, offered an escape from the harsh reality of life, especially in the overcrowded and cheerless houses of the slum areas.

To add to the attraction of alcoholic drinks, the landlords were not slow to add some entertainment. Those which provided such were known as 'free and easies'. Patrons who could sing (or thought they could) were encouraged to do so. The more talented were able to perform for payment or at least free refreshment. Some would have a small stage for performers and others a separate room. 'Artistes' became more professional, often travelling from town to town. An observer under the name of 'Asmodeus' visited one of them in 1860 and wrote a lurid account of the proceedings:

There were women, or things attired like them, in their behaviour and in their language obscene mingling with men half drunk whose conversation formed a fitting adjunct to the pandemonium.

The entertainment was appropriate for such a place.

Later in the century, the entertainment became a little more refined and new buildings were erected with better facilities, which became known as music halls, with the sort of performances the BBC used to recreate under the title *The Good Old Days*.

One such music hall in Nottingham was built in 1854, known as St George's Hall at the west end of Parliament Street. One of the earliest appearances there was of Vesta Tilley at the age of six. The Hall was demolished in 1900 when Parliament Street needed to be widened.

Other music halls were opened in Nottingham in the last quarter of the nineteenth century, including a Temperance one. In 1898 the Nottingham Empire was opened on North Sherwood Street. An early act here was 'Eight Lancashire Lads', including the ten-year old Charlie Chaplin. Other famous names from the widening variety of music hall turns followed. The invention of radio brought a new form of entertainment by enabling those only heard on the 'wireless' to be seen as well, including some of the well-known dance

St George's Hall made Parliament Street so narrow at its end that it was demolished.

bands. After the Second World War, talking films, some in colour, and later television, caused a falling off of demand. Despite efforts to keep up with the times, The Empire was demolished in 1968 to make way for the new Concert Hall.

NEWS HOUSES

The industrialisation of England in the early nineteenth century was accompanied by a growing demand from the working class for more information about public affairs. In Nottingham, as elsewhere, newspapers were well established, but the cost to workers was prohibitive for them to buy. Accordingly, a custom grew up of some public houses allowing more literate persons to read out aloud some of the more interesting items.

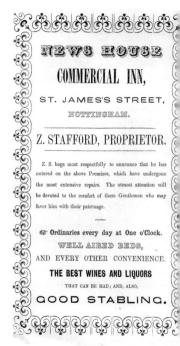

Pigot and Company's Directory for 1828–29 contains a list of public houses in Nottingham and it names two of them as *News Houses*. One was on St James Street and the other on Canal Street. Both still survive although the actual buildings will have been renewed from time to time. The one on Canal Street still retains the same name but the St James Street one has been renamed *Bar Oz*. It does, however, have an information board giving the history of news houses.

In the 1930s there was a different News House on Upper Parliament Street. This was a cinema, which specialised in short programmes of newsreels, documentary films and cartoons. It retained its character until the 1960s when it was demolished but changed its name several times including the Odd Hour Cinema.

This advertisement appeared in 1848. The Commercial Inn is still there bu[t] renamed Bar Oz.

NEWSPAPERS

National, or more accurately London, newspapers were published from the early eighteenth century. In Nottingham the first newspaper was probably the *Weekly Courant* issued by William Ayscough in 1712. Its name was changed to the *Nottingham Weekly Courant* until 1769 when on a change of ownership it became the *Nottingham Journal*, a title it retained until the 1960s when it was amalgamated with the *Nottingham Guardian*, as the *Guardian-Journal*. The *Guardian* was first produced in 1846.

Other newspapers appeared from time to time in the eighteenth century, but most were short-lived. Much of these early newspapers consisted of copies of the London papers with news of policies and foreign affairs, although they did include some local news. When Charles Sutton produced the *Nottingham Review* in 1808, it challenged the hitherto supporter of Tory politics, the *Nottingham Journal*, by a support of Whig or Reform Politics. These two, together with the *Nottingham and Newark Mercury* provided more local news and opinions for most of the first half of the nineteenth century. The *Review* ceased in 1870, when two daily newspapers caused its circulation to fall. These were the *Nottingham Daily Express* (1859) and the *Nottingham Guardian* which also became a daily in 1861. Evening papers started in the 1880s, the *Guardian* proprietors creating the *Evening Post* with the *Journal* publishing the *Evening News*. Both groups also produced sporting papers and the *Guardian* had a weekly edition.

The entrance to the Express offices, designed by Watson Fothergill remains. It was used for the Nottingham Daily Express *later for the* Nottingham Journal *and the* Evening News.

The growth of radio and television as providers of up to date news first of all forced the amalgamation of the two morning papers, which even so could not compete with popular national morning papers. The *Evening News* also ceased publication leaving the *Evening Post* as the only surviving Nottingham newspaper.

The early twentieth century saw the publication of weekly newspapers for suburban areas, such as Beeston and Bulwell. Some have survived or have been converted to the ranks of free papers.

NOTTINGHAM EXPRESS TRANSIT

After some years of discussion and negotiation, an Act of Parliament was obtained in 1992 to allow a modern tramway system to be constructed on similar lines to recent ones at Sheffield and Manchester. Line One was commenced in 1994 to provide a service from Station Street to Hucknall with stations at Hyson Green, Basford and Bulwell, and a spur to Cinderhill. The actual construction works caused problems with traffic in the city centre and especially at Hyson Green where trade at shops was affected.

It was hoped to open the line to passengers in November 2003, but technical problems caused postponement to March 2004. From October 2003 onwards

This is the tram stop in the Old Market Square for the southbound line.

the trams became a familiar sight in the city as testing the system and training of drivers took place. It became fully operational in March 2004.

O'CONNOR, FEARGUS

Born in County Cork, Ireland, in 1794, Feargus O'Connor studied at Trinity College, Dublin, and became a lawyer. He was elected as a Member of Parliament in 1832, for the constituency of County Cork, as Ireland was then still part of the United Kingdom. After he was unseated as a member in 1835 he devoted his time to the Chartist movement. He first came to Nottingham in November 1836 whilst on a tour of the Midlands. He soon became one of the leaders of the Chartists and on a visit to Nottingham in February 1842, he was treated to a triumphant entry by his supporters. He took an active part in the events leading up to a Parliamentary by-election in March, an election noted for its rowdiness and violence. He described his part in fighting, which took place as 'flooring his opponents like nine pins'. He

Feargus O'Connor's statue still stands in the Arboretum whilst many other Nottingham MPs have no such memorial.

achieved fame in 1847 when he was elected as one of two MPs in that year, thus becoming the only Chartist to become an MP. He was elected along with John Walter junior, in a unique collaboration due to the Tories seeking revenge over their treatment by the Whigs who repudiated an agreement on voting.

O'Connor also was the main force behind a movement known as his land plan, which sought to raise money in a kind of co-operative society to buy land and help the unemployed become small holders. The scheme was not a success, nor was O'Connor's career in the House of Commons. His conduct was eccentric but was explained when he was declared insane.

After his death in 1855, some of his supporters erected a statue to him in the Arboretum. Even in death he remained a controversial figure. A petition to the Council opposing the erection of the statue stated that there was nothing in his public character and principles to entitle him to have a statue.
☛ *See also Chartism*

PARK, NOTTINGHAM

To Nottingham's residents 'The Park' means only one thing, an exclusive residential privately owned suburb adjoining Nottingham Castle. It has been so described since the beginning of the nineteenth century. Before that, for nearly eight hundred years, it had been a royal forest and from the late

This is one of the Park entrances, which can be closed to establish its rights as a private estate.

seventeenth century onwards the property of the Dukes of Newcastle.

When Nottingham Castle was built by William Peverel as a royal defence and residence, the land to the west became the park, with deer and other game for the pleasure of royalty and their guests on their visits to the castle. After the civil wars of the seventeenth century, the castle was demolished and the site became the property of the Duke of Newcastle, who erected the ducal mansion, which is now the home of Nottingham's Castle Museum and Art Gallery.

Subsequent Dukes of Newcastle had other residences and seldom lived in the castle, which in any case became a roofless ruin after it was burned down by rioters in 1831, until restored by the Borough as the Castle Museum.

In the mid nineteenth century the Duke of Newcastle decided to develop the bowl shaped land of the former royal park as a residential estate. A master plan of the layout was drawn up and carried out to the design, which it is today. The houses erected were large architect designed with gardens and stables, which only the relatively wealthy could afford. The main building period was the second half of the nineteenth century and the owners included most of Nottingham's leading manufacturers and industrialists, magistrates, aldermen, mayors and officials.

The ownership later became vested in a trust for the benefit of Oxford University and the exclusive private nature of the Park remains with gates, which can close off roads to demonstrate its privacy. Most of the houses are now too large for smaller families and some have been converted into flats. Some newer dwellings have been built and The Park is now a conservation area.

PARKS AND RECREATION GROUNDS

Public parks and recreation grounds are an innovation of the nineteenth century. In its 1845 Enclosure Act, Nottingham set aside land for the establishment of the Arboretum, the Forest on the edge of the town, a cricket ground in the Meadows and tree-lined walks known as Queens Walk, Meadows, and Elm Avenue, Corporation Oaks and Robin Hood Chase in St Anns. This showed considerable enlightenment for the period and it was followed by the Corporation in 1868 when it appointed a Public Walks and Recreation Grounds Committee. This did nor result in further developments at first, but when the Borough was enlarged in 1877, consideration had to be given to similar facilities in the added areas such as Bulwell and Sneinton. The Council seemed quite unaware of the irony of re-naming its Committee the Public Parks and Burial Grounds Committee, although did help to create small islands of grass in some of the disused burial grounds. Lenton Recreation Ground was opened in 1889 and similar parks, with grassed areas surrounded by iron loops, with notices 'Keep Off The Grass' created.

It was not until the twentieth century that Nottingham started to expand its provision of public open spaces. It was then that three established large

This was a lodge to one of Nottingham's earliest parks on Millstone Lane (now Huntingdon Street).

houses with extensive grounds became available and were acquired by the Corporation to use as parks. These were Bulwell Hall, Woodthorpe Grange and the Lenton Estate, which became the site of the University College and the adjoining Highfields Parks. The main 'jewel' was the purchase of Wollaton Hall and its parkland, which was then partly outside the City but came within it in 1933.

Other parks and recreation grounds were added from time to time, especially in the expanded areas and council house estates. Cricket pitches, football grounds, bowling greens, tennis courts and pitch and putt courses became popular and children's playgrounds with swings and other attractions contributed to Nottingham's deserved reputation as a 'green' City.

PEOPLE'S COLLEGE

In 1846 the People's College was erected on College Street to provide more advanced education at a moderate fee for pupils who had already received basic education. The building was paid for by a public subscription, towards which George Gill made a considerable donation. He had also been instrumental in promoting the idea of such a school.

Gill was a wealthy former textile manufacturer. He was born in 1778 and played a part in public affairs being Sheriff in 1816. He made a number of other benefactions and in recognition of this Gill Street was named in his honour.

The college taught subjects which were later undertaken by the University College. The school buildings, with a number of extensions were taken over by the Nottingham School Board and re-named the Ropewalk School, one department having its entrance on the Ropewalk. It then became vested in the City Council's Education Committee. The Committee continued to call

This plaque is on the College Street side of the building.

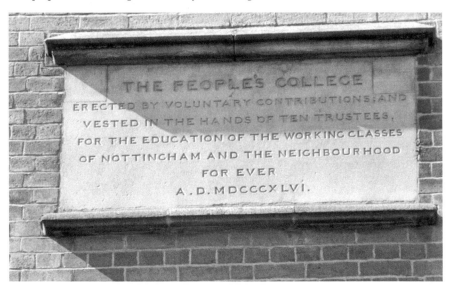

the Ropewalk site by that name, but re-named the College Street site as the Peoples College for Senior Boys. After the Second World War it became a school for training pupils for the building trades. A new People's College of Further Education was also set up, which moved to a new building on Maid Marian Way. The College Street and Ropewalk buildings were transferred to the Workers' Education Association for overflow adult classes from the Association's Shakespeare Street building.

PHOTOGRAPHY

The first public demonstration of photography took place in Paris in 1839. The images became known as daguerreotypes after its main inventor, Louis Daguerre. The method immediately became popular as an alternative to portrait painting. Nottingham was to have an early professional photographer, Alfred Barber who was a local bookseller and printer. He obtained a lease on attic rooms at Bromley House on Angel Row. He had to make complex and expensive alterations to enable him to use daylight to take photographs.

The studio opened on 2 October 1841, but Barber was only able to operate until January 1843 because of legal difficulties, which resulted in an injunction stopping him working. He had managed to take £53 and made a profit of £19. The cost of photographic portraits was relatively expensive, up to £1, which was more than most weekly wages. The process involved some difficulties with ladies clothing and Barber had to specify which materials were suitable.

The Bromley House studio remained empty for three years, when a Hungarian, George Popowitz, started the business again. He was able to offer portraits at 7s 6d (32.5p), still beyond the means of most families. The premises at Bromley House continued to be used for photography until 1955.

Technical improvements and increased prosperity in the nineteenth century enabled photography to expand in Nottingham and there were over 300 professional photographers working in the City between 1841–1910. This illustrates how popular the habit of having one's photograph taken became.

Portraits were not, however, the only use of photography. Outdoor scenes were taken as early as the 1860s and the era of picture postcards from about 1900 resulted in hundreds of views of Nottingham places.

Further information on the history of photography in Nottinghamshire can be found in *Pioneers of Photography in Nottinghamshire 1841–1910* by Bernard and Pauline Heathcote. This, their latest publication, includes a bibliography of twenty-one works, most of them by Pauline Heathcote.

☛ *See also Amateur Photography*

POLICE

When Nottingham was a town of a few thousand people, the enforcement of law and order was more of a community responsibility. The town was divided into wards with a decennary for each one, an unpaid constable. One of the seven aldermen was allocated to each ward and in 1635 it was ordered that:

> *every Alderman shall, once a fortnight, with the assistance of some of his ward, walk his ward to see what strangers or inmates do come in, that some course be taken to remove them.*

An Act of Parliament in 1285, the Statute of Winchester, gave towns the power to introduce the Watch and Ward system. The Watch was the night duty of the watchmen and Ward the daytime.

This became particularly important in Nottingham in the early part of the nineteenth century during periods of unrest mainly due to the poverty of the working classes and such episodes as the Luddite machine breaking. The Corporation could at such times call upon all able bodied men to serve as watchmen, to supplement the work of the few full time paid watchmen. In 1812 the Town Clerk, a solicitor who was paid for any work he carried out, submitted an account for £22.7s for summoning 894 persons to Watch and Ward and attending the Watch every night from 28 April to 10 June. Ninety-seven constables and their assistants, who were of course unpaid, did receive some recompense, £2.8s.6d.

The Municipal Reform Act 1835 required the new elected council to appoint a Watch Committee which agreed to set up a full time paid police force. By 1844 the council was concerned about the cost compared with the £1 per day in 1833. The cost of the Chief Constable, 1 Superintendent, 5 Inspectors and 42 Policemen was eight times as much, nearly £3,000 a year. This was more than half the borough rate.

The police force was not slow in taking advantage of new methods of carrying out their work. In 1859 it spent £11.6s.6d on photographic apparatus and in 1881 telephonic communication with other departments was established. From 1874 onwards the Watch Committee submitted an annual report to the Council, with the Chief Constable's report. The first one gave the numbers of the police force, which included 16 sergeants and 96 constables. Property stolen in the year was valued at £633, but £303 worth was recovered. There had been an outbreak of vandalism on an evening in February when a gang of youths rampaged through the town, breaking windows and damaging property. As soon as police arrived the gangs dispersed, leaving the Chief Constable to complain that policemen, dressed in long heavy greatcoats, and tired after a long day could not be expected to follow active young men. He did, however, say that they eventually convicted the ringleader.

The report for 1898–99 gave a four year statement of statistics showing how in several categories crimes had decreased. Indictable offences fell from

780 to 620, drunkenness from 1,627 to 1,488 and juvenile offenders from 205 to 143. Of these 2 were sent to reformatory schools, 15 to industrial schools and 5 were whipped. Lost children seemed to have been a major problem, as high as 4,102 in one year.

Reports in the twentieth century were quite optimistic, commenting that compared with other places, Nottingham suffered little serious crime. The 1930s saw some major new techniques in policing with radios in police cars and a forensic science laboratory.

The annual report for 1959 presented a very different picture. The Chief Constable reported that the previous three years had seen a vast and increasing number of crimes, so much so that he asked for an additional number of staff of 67 people.

The City Police Force ceased to exist from April 1967, when it merged with the County force to form the Nottinghamshire Combined Police Authority.

POST OFFICE

Wright's Directory for 1832 commented that the Post Office on High Street 'has long been too small and inconvenient of its business'. This was in the days before penny postage, when the recipient of a letter had to pay for it. The Royal Mail had been in existence since 1660, with a fleet of stagecoaches, which left London every night carrying bags of mail to all parts of the country. These were deposited in towns, at post offices, for delivery locally. In 1832 the Nottingham office was open from 7am to 10pm, from April to October, closing at 8pm the rest of the year. George Keppel White was the postmaster and his two letter carriers were sent out on delivery at 8.30am, 11am and 2.30pm.

On 10 January 1840 penny postage started. This was to be of considerable benefit to the lace and hosiery trades in

This was Nottingham's second post office, on Old Queen Street (now Fletcher Gate) until the buildings were erected on the (new) Queen Street site in the 1890s.

Nottingham as previously the charge was 5d to Derby and 10d (4p) to London. The High Street office continued to be used but in December 1846 the Town Council appointed a committee to consider the desirableness of removing the Post Office to a new site. This was done, the new office being built at the corner of Albert Street, which had just been constructed to join Wheeler Gate to Lister Gate. In 1869 the Post Office moved to Victoria Street where it remained until 1897 when the new Queen and King Streets were constructed. The building it occupied is now used for other purposes, the Post Office removing to its present site at the top of Queen Street.

QUAKERS

Quakers or the Society of Friends, were one of the seventeenth century religious groups opposed to the Church of England doctrines, which were prevented from meeting under the Conventicle Acts. There were about 100 of them in the town in 1669 and they have always remained a small but influential group.

The new Society of Friends premises were built in the 1960s on Clarendon Street to replace the previous Meeting House on Friar Lane.

One of their members, Samuel Fox, was well-known in early nineteenth century as a philanthropist and supporter of education. He owned land at the bottom of St Ann's Well Road which he gave to form a burial ground, which became known as Fox's Close.

The Society of Friends had its first meeting-house in Nottingham on Friar Lane (when it was known as Park Street) from 1847 to the 1960s when it was demolished. Its premises were then transferred to a new modern building on Clarendon Street, adjoining its own burial ground.

QUARTER SESSIONS

From 1449 the Royal Charter provided that the seven Aldermen should also be the justices of the peace for the borough. They administered justice, both civil and criminal, through the Borough Court or Petty Sessions. They also met quarterly to deal with more serious crimes and also with certain civil matters such as registration of friendly societies and of freemasons. The Borough Quarter Sessions were independent of the similar court in the county after 1449.

Under the Municipal Corporations Act 1835 Nottingham continued to have a Court of Quarter Sessions, which did not have the close connection with the Corporation that it had previously, as aldermen were no longer automatically justices of the peace.

The establishment of Crown Courts in the twentieth century resulted in the abolition of both Quarter Sessions and Assizes.

RADFORD

The Anglo-Saxon settlements of Radford and Lenton were close to each other on the River Leen and would have had similar economies. After the Norman invasion, when in the twelfth century Lenton Priory was established, Radford became the poor relation. Small pockets of Radford were given to Lenton, which later caused a certain amount of administrative difficulty.

After the dissolution of Lenton Priory, life in the two parishes would have once again been similar. The establishment in the late eighteenth century of the textile industry in and around the borough resulted in some of the adjoining parishes becoming similarly industrialised. This was the case with both Lenton and Radford, but in very different ways. Lenton covered 5,080 acres compared with Radford's 1,000, yet the latter's population was, in 1801, 2,269 as against Lenton's 893. It continued to grow in population due, as *White's Directory* (of 1832) explained that 'it has drank so deeply of the manufacturing spirit' of Nottingham. It was the second largest parish in the county, with a greater population than Newark. It is not difficult to understand why as one point of Radford, near Canning Circus, was only half

A typical street scene of nineteenth century development, with houses and factories near each other.

a mile from the Old Market Square. *White's Directory* added that 1,100 new houses had been built in the last ten years and 'form several handsome villages, occupied chiefly by bobbin net makers'.

By 1871 its population was over 15,000 but although it was a Union with a Board of Guardians it had no Local Board of Health and no Medical Officer of Health. In 1871 there was a prevalence of typhoid fever in the parish and the Privy Council sent Dr Thorne to investigate. His report was so critical of the living conditions that he was sent back a year later to see what improvements had been made. The short answer was – not many. However, the message seemed to have had one effect – the setting up of a Local Board and the appointment of a Medical Officer.

When a Local Board was set up it was short lived as Radford was incorporated into the Borough in 1877.

Apart from the insanitary conditions, which caused diseases, the worst feature of Radford was the serious overcrowding of such a large population in a small area. No wonder the City Council's Housing Committee visited Radford as its first inspection.

The general appearance of Radford was little changed from the nineteenth century as late as the 1950s. The resumption of post-1945 slum clearance on a large scale started with the Denman Street area. Unfortunately, at that time it was not thought practicable to demolish buildings other than houses. The result is still visible in parts of the area such as around Boden Street where industrial buildings predominate. The redevelopment of the cleared areas was marked by the first high rise municipal flats in the City. These were not too popular and one block has since been demolished.

Radford also included Hyson Green, where following a clearance scheme, a new form of housing, 'deck-access', was built. These too have been demolished because of defects and general unpopularity with tenants.

RADIO AND TELEVISION

The term wireless gradually gave way to the term radio and with the setting up of the British Broadcasting Corporation's network of national and regional stations, Nottingham's 5GB was discontinued.

The introduction of FM (frequency modulation) stations in the 1950s was followed by the re-introduction of a Nottingham Service, Radio Nottingham starting up in 1968 from premises in York House, Mansfield Road. In 1998 a new purpose-built centre was erected on London Road for both radio and television, the latter being re-introduced nationally in the late 1940s. At first reception was through the H-type aerials which became a symbol of some affluence.

Independent radio and television paid for by advertisements came to Nottingham through Radio Trent, with premises on Castle Gate and a large television studio on Lenton Lane.

☛ *See also Wireless*

RAILWAYS – NINETEENTH CENTURY

In 1832 a group of colliery owners met at the *Sun Inn*, Eastwood and decided to form a new railway to be called the Midland Counties Railway. The purpose of the line was to move minerals, coal, stone and iron ore, from the Derbyshire/Nottingham coalfield down the Erewash Valley to connect with Leicestershire and the West Midlands. Nottingham men were in the minority who subscribed the capital, which had an unfortunate result, as Derby seized the initiative and Nottingham was left with only a branch line to Derby. This even today puts Nottingham at a disadvantage, especially for passenger traffic.

The Nottingham station was on the south bank of the canal, where today the Magistrates' Court is. This was the first incursion into the Meadows and was the forerunner of other physical changes including a bridge over the canal at Carrington Street, new roads and for a time a level crossing.

Nottingham's second railway station was near London Road and the adjoining street was imaginatively named Station Street.

The railway amalgamated with other companies and became the Midland Railway. In 1840 the line was extended eastwards to Lincoln and a new station opened on Station Street. In 1848 another new line went through Lenton and Radford and thence to Mansfield via Basford and Bulwell. This line then branched past Radford to join the main line from Derby to Alfreton and the north.

Another company was formed with the longest title but the shortest stretch. Named the Ambergate, Nottingham and Boston and Eastern Junction, the only stretch built was from Colwick to Grantham. This involved building a new station on London Road, designed by T C Hine, when the Great Northern Railway took over the former company. The Great Northern also had a line from Colwick and Netherfield, which went by a circuitous route to Derbyshire, via Gedling and Daybrook with just one station in Nottingham, *Basford and Bulwell* on Highbury Road.

The Midland Railway then opened a new route to London, via Melton Mowbray and Oakham to Marylebone. This involved building bridges over Meadow Lane and the River Trent, with five more in West Bridgford. Another short-lived railway was the Nottingham Suburban, which linked two stretches of the Great Northern Railway, with stations at Thorneywood, St Ann's and Sherwood. It had engineering problems with gradients but its demise owed something to competition from the electric tramway system from 1901 and the line effectively ceased in 1916.

The last decades of the nineteenth century saw the building of the Manchester, Sheffield and Lincolnshire line through North Nottinghamshire. It entered the city at Bulwell with stations at Bulwell Forest, Haydn Road and Carrington. From there it went through a tunnel, emerging at what in 1901 became Victoria Station.

RAILWAYS – TWENTIETH CENTURY
The Manchester, Sheffield and Lincolnshire line was renamed the Great Central Railway as Victoria Station was a joint venture with the Great Northern. The new line, especially the station, made a considerable

When the Great Central railway tunnelled its way from Victoria Station, it emerged at Weekday Cross and property to the south including this scene at the junction of Red Lion Street and Sussex Street was demolished.

difference to Nottingham's appearance. The tunnel from Carrington started from a level lower than that of the surface of Milton Street where the station was. This meant that considerable excavation was needed for the track. There was a bonus for the City in this, as it involved what was the biggest slum clearance up to then. All houses, public houses, churches and chapels disappeared and the new station platforms were reached down steps.

The trains ran under Parliament Street and through another tunnel to Weekday Cross. At its exit one line turned eastwards to join the Great Northern line to Colwick and onwards, including King's Cross. The main line to London crossed Canal Street, Station Street, the Midland Railway and Arkwright Street, where there was a station. From there the line crossed the Meadows on embankments, with a bridge over the river at Wilford. From there it went via Ruddington, East Leake, Loughborough and Leicester to London.

The Midland Railway, not to be outdone, built a new station on Carrington Street. In the 1920s the multiplicity of small companies became rationalised, the Midland Railway becoming part of the London Midland and Scottish group, whilst the Great Northern and Great Central joined the London and North Eastern.

The nineteenth century had seen the rise of railways, with peak freight and passenger figures in the 1920s. The second half of the twentieth century saw the decline of the railways following nationalisation into British Rail. Due mainly to other means of transport, Dr Beeching was commissioned to deliver the death sentence. Whole networks were closed and railway stations and other buildings demolished.

Nottingham was left with only the Midland Station. Victoria like its predecessors of sixty years earlier disappeared and the 'hole' filled with the Victoria Centre Shopping Mall, car parks and a towering block of flats. The LMS line through the Leen Valley was retained for freight but in the 1990s was restored for passenger use as far as Worksop.

Diesel engines replaced steam, but electrification has not reached Nottingham because of technical problems.

RALEIGH

When the Sandfield open field was developed under the Enclosure Act, new streets were made to connect Alfreton Road with what became Waverley Street. One of these was named Raleigh Street and leading off was Walter Street. In 1881, a directory listed, between numbers 13 and 15 Raleigh Works, Robert B Gamble, bobbin and carriage maker. By 1885, Richard J Ball, described as cycle machinist, was also occupying the premises. In 1887 Ball's place was occupied by Woodhead and Angois, cycle and general machinists. In the alphabetical section Woodhead was Richard Maurice and

Frank Bowden, in addition to his cycle interests undertook public duties including laying this foundation stone for the new Salvation Army building on King Edward Street.

Angois was Paul, living at Russell Street. The partnership name also included a William Ellis who was also a lace gasser. Two years later the firm had moved to nearby Russell Street. In 1893 the Russell Street premises were in the possession of the Raleigh Cycle Company Limited, Frank Bowden, chairman and managing director. The directory of that year had, for the first time, a heading in the trade section of 'cycle machinists and dealers' of whom there were thirty-six.

Frank Bowden had been in the Far East but had returned to England for health reasons. He had been advised to take up the new cycling, which he did and also took over the firm of Woodhead and Angois. He was made a baronet for his charitable work and built the Raleigh Cycle Company up to become one of the City's largest employers. His son, Sir Harold carried on the business, which was eventually absorbed into Tube Investments. The cycle works has completely severed its connections with Nottingham, the University of Nottingham's Jubilee Campus being erected on part of the former Faraday Road site.

RELIGIOUS CENSUS OF 1851

The decennial census of 1851, compiled on the basis of persons resident on 30 March, was accompanied by another one. The religious census to be completed for each place of worship had forms to be signed by the incumbent or some person who had a connection with the place. The return required information as to the number of people who could be accommodated and the number present on the census day. These were to show separately the congregation at the services – morning, afternoon and evening – showing adults and scholars separately. The return also asked for an estimate of the average attendances for the same categories over the previous twelve months. The difficulty of obtaining accurate numbers for such a novel exercise can be gathered and in particular many returns have no estimate of the previous twelve months average.

Nevertheless, analysis of the returns for the whole country revealed that only about 40 per cent of the adult population attended a place of worship. This was a shock to the government and ecclesiastics, and there was controversy about the method of carrying out the census. As a result the experiment was never repeated.

In 1988 the University of Nottingham Department of Adult Education published in two volumes *The Religious Census of 1851* for the whole of the county of Nottingham. This has been edited by Michael Watts and gives a transcript of each of the original returns for every place of worship, listed by parishes but with the returns in each one for every denomination. There are also a number of tables summarising the numbers of worshippers in various categories.

The returns also give the date when the church, chapel or other building was established and the name and status of the compilers. In Nottingham 42.4% of the 58,419 population were worshippers, 14.8 per cent were Church of England and 24.1 per cent non-conformists. Three per cent were Roman Catholics and 0.7 per cent Latter Day Saints/Mormons. Separate figures are given for six districts, which became part of the Borough in 1877. These show 21 per cent of the population as non-conformists and about 10 per cent Church of England. The latter is estimated, as there was no return for Lenton Parish Church.

The returns also show that in the borough the numbers of Methodists was only a few more than what is described as 'Old Dissenters' – e.g. Baptists and Independents. In the other districts the position was much different with more than twice the number of Methodists over Old Dissenters.

One rather surprising position was at Sneinton where there was a population of 8,440. Apart from the parish church there was only one other denomination, Refuge (Independents) with a building used for other purposes as well and only accommodating 70 people.

The Borough had 39 places of worship, all of course within the confined boundaries around the market place, as the effect of the Enclosure Act had not started to result in new churches. The Church of England had nine places

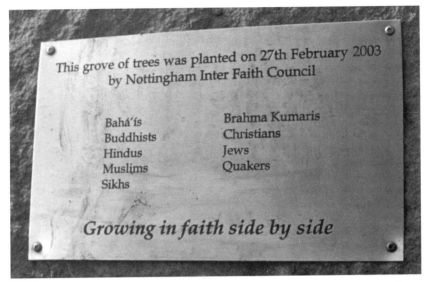

This inter-faith plaque in Bath Street Rest Garden shows the changes in faiths since 1850.

of worship, including the three ancient parish churches and four, which had been built since 1800. There were two other buildings used temporarily. These were the cemetery chapel on Bath Street and a schoolroom on Derby Road. The main non-conformist chapels of Baptist, Methodist and Independents had seven each, with the various sectarian differences. The Roman Catholics still had a church on George Street but this had not been used since St Barnabas had been erected in 1844.

The Jews, Society of Friends and Latter Day Saints each had one place and there were four others including Swedenborgians and Huntingtonians whilst the Salem Chapel on Barker Gate was described as 'Disciples of Jesus Christ or Christians'.

The Catholic and Apostolic Church sent its return in but gave no information in protest against being classed under any sectarian name. The form was signed by Cuthbert Orlebar, Angel or Bishop of the Church.

ROBIN HOOD RIFLES

In 1859, the Government was alarmed by threats of invasion by France and called for volunteers to form rifle companies, which could if necessary assist the regular army. Nottingham responded to a call from the Lord Lieutenant, the Duke of Newcastle, to form such a body, which was given the name of Robin Hood Rifles. Among the first volunteers was A J Mundella, who later

The former orderly room in the Castle grounds now does duty as a store.

became a MP and President of the Board of Education, G T Hine, brother of T C Hine, the architect and several men who later became Mayor of Nottingham including Richard Birkin and William Lambert.

Several companies were formed and they used the Castle grounds for parades with a building as orderly room, which later became a garden store. The men were given uniforms and had annual camps and training. A rifle range was provided at Coppice Farm. This was closed in 1898 on orders from the War Office as it was considered too dangerous. A new one was built near Trent Station, Long Eaton.

When the Boer War broke out in 1899, the British Army called for volunteers from the rifle clubs. Thirty men of the Robin Hood Rifles, together with others from Derbyshire became part of a brigade, which fought in South Africa. In 1910, the British Army was re-formed with the Territorial Army established for part-time volunteer soldiers. Rifle clubs and similar units were amalgamated with regiments, the Robin Hood Rifles becoming the Robin Hood Battalion of the Sherwood Foresters.

SHERIFFS

In his Charter of 1449, King Henry VI gave Nottingham the right to appoint two Sheriffs from among themselves instead of the town bailiffs. The Charter of 1284, which gave Nottingham the right to have a Mayor, also granted the right to appoint two bailiffs, one for each of the two Boroughs, English and French. Thomas Bailey in his *Annals of Nottinghamshire* wrote that Robin Hood, the outlaw, died in 1247, so his tussles with the Sheriff of Nottingham could hardly have been with the two, or even one of them, appointed annually from 1449. The Sheriff in question was the Crown's tax-gather for Nottinghamshire and Derbyshire and as such not altogether popular.

The two Sheriffs formed part of the ruling body of Mayor, Aldermen and Council, together with other officers, which were created to deal with specific matters such as the Free School and the Bridge Estate. After their year of office they became part of the Clothing or Livery. This was a waiting list from which new aldermen were recruited when a vacancy arose.

The Sheriffs were responsible for certain financial matters and some part of the judicial system. By the seventeenth century part of the legal duties required use of qualified lawyers or attorneys. The Council elected Sheriff's Clerks and Sergeants. As these became more numerous, they were paid fees. Eventually they became known as Under-Sheriffs. One duty, which the Sheriffs were no doubt pleased to delegate to the Under-Sheriff was witnessing hangings of miscreants from the town's courts.

Under the Municipal Reform Act 1835, Nottingham was allowed to continue appointing one Sheriff. The town retained the two maces, which it had and these are still placed before the City Council at its formal meetings. The early Sheriffs after 1835 were usually not existing councillors or aldermen but later it became the usual practice to appoint Sheriffs from these existing members. The duties are now mostly ceremonial and supplement those carried out by the Lord Mayor and Deputy Lord Mayor.

SHERWOOD FOREST

What, it may be asked, has Nottingham to do with Sherwood Forest? The answer in 1609, at least, is to be found in a Crown survey carried out by Richard Bankes in that year. The result has been *Sherwood Forest in 1609* a transcript published by the Thoroton Society of Nottinghamshire in 1997. The survey itself and accompanying maps have been transcribed meticulously by Stephanos Mastoris and Sue Groves. The publication has two plates of the original survey and map, which indicate the amount of work needed to put them in readable order.

Sherwood Forest was a royal forest, which was left in medieval times as a place for hunting by the monarch and his followers and was subject to forest law. The survey shows the boundaries of the forest, in the south the River Trent north bank, extending to Clumber in the north. It encompassed forty-six lordships in a rough oval shape with a narrowing in the centre. It thus included Nottingham and the adjoining areas, which later became part of the borough. The purpose of the survey was to show who were the owners and the tenants of the various lands, with a view to establishing what income was due to the Crown. Because it was called 'Forest' did not mean that it was complete and continuous woodland. It was, to some extent, in central Nottinghamshire because of the sandy soil and this part was famous for its oak trees, few of which survive.

As far as Nottingham borough is concerned the chief interest is the extent to which the open fields are shown. It is also interesting for the Leen Valley settlements showing their dependence on the river.

SNEINTON

In Domesday Book, Sneinton is named as 'Notintone' and the derivation is the 'tun' of the personal name, which in the case of the adjoining borough of Nottingham, Snotingeham, ingeham meaning the people of the farm (-ham) of Snot. Why the 'S' was dropped for Notintone and not for Snotingeham is not clear. It is supposed that the Normans had difficulty in pronouncing Sn. The 'S' was restored for other early documents and has been retained ever since, although the spelling was for many years 'Snenton'.

Like the other areas around Nottingham, which became part of the Borough in 1877, Sneinton shared in the expansion of the textile industry of the late eighteenth century. This is not surprising as even the original site was only half a mile from Nottingham's St Mary's Church. It was a daughter church of St Mary's until 1831.

Queen Adelaide *public house stood in isolation after most of the properties around it had been demolished. A new house of the same name was erected on Windmill Lane.*

Like Radford, in the first decades of the nineteenth century, Sneinton expanded with a number of separated hamlets, Old Sneinton, New Sneinton, Middle Sneinton, Element Hill and Hermitage. The parish had a boundary with the River Trent, in the latter's northern bank, east of Trent Bridge. The population had increased to 12,237 by 1871, from 3,567 in 1831.

Following the amalgamation with the borough, Sneinton continued to expand, gradually filling in the gaps between the former hamlets. It remained an industrial suburb, with hosiery and lace factories. In the twentieth century it gradually became more residential but largely a working class suburb. The Edwardian era saw an extension eastwards with the making of Sneinton Dale and later the extension of Colwick Road which until then had been a toll road to Netherfield. In the 1930s Sneinton Dale was extended to Bakersfield with the creation of council housing estates including a small extension into Carlton.

Slum clearance began in the 1930s and continued in the 1960s, the latter creating a site for three multi-storey blocks of flats.

Two of Sneinton's famous 'sons' are remembered by the statue of General William Booth at the Salvation Army Centre, which has retained his birthplace, whilst George Green, a mathematician ahead of his time has his windmill restored to working order.

SPORT

Nottingham has enjoyed a variety of sports, the earliest probably being archery. Butt Dyke (now Park Row) was known by that name as early as the thirteenth century. The archers would practice there as a means of being prepared for war and reports refer to wagering on the contests. Other medieval sports would include cock-fighting, bull and bear-baiting as spectator sports. Pugilism in the nineteenth century, as practiced by Bendigo gave way to more refined boxing with gloves on when it became regarded as a healthy exercise for schoolboys.

Cricket became an organised sport in the eighteenth century when the counties started to play each other. The Forest was used as a racecourse and cricket started there before William Clarke started what was to become a world famed Test match ground, just outside the City boundary.

Football of a sort was no doubt played for centuries but only became organised in 1862 when the first Nottingham Club, Notts County was formed followed three years later by Nottingham Forest. The second half of the nineteenth century saw greater active participation by working class men (at first) in football and cricket with local leagues. The River Trent became useful both for rowing and swimming. Up to 1939, regular swimming contests took place in the river. Cycling became popular towards the end of the nineteenth century mainly for the middle classes, as a machine would cost several months wages of a workingman. Ladies too became cyclists.

Ice skating became an indoor sport in Nottingham in 1938 when the Ice Stadium was built. The Panthers Ice Hockey team had its base there.

The twentieth century saw a considerable expansion in other sports, such as golf, tennis, rugby football, athletics, bowls and croquet. Spectator sports also included speedway/motorcycles, greyhound racing and all-in wrestling. The City Council and major employers provided sports grounds and facilities and indoor sports became organised as mentioned in 'Mechanics Institutes'. Ice skating indoors started in the City in the 1930s and has led to the new and enlarged centre inspired by the success of Torvill and Dean.

More recent developments have included squash courts, gymnasia, indoor bowling, martial arts and a national tennis centre, in a world which has seen sport become a major industry.

SUBSIDY ROLLS

In 1473, the Crown required the town of Nottingham to assess the income arising from all the freehold properties and to collect one-tenth of the amount from the freeholder. The list, which has survived gives the names of the 154 freeholders and the amount they had to pay. This is a large number of freeholders and reflects how the town had grown into a community of freemen, rather than the subjects of one wealthy landowner. The amounts payable range from 2¹/2d to £3-14s-7¹/2d. The latter was payable by Thomas Thurland, nine times mayor of Nottingham and who was mainly responsible for re-building St Mary's Church. There were only seven others who paid more than £1 and at the other end of the scale most paid less than 10/- (50p) each.

Another subsidy, in 1524, has a roll, which gives the names of the streets in which the people lived. There are eighteen streets, the names of which apart from four are the same as they are today, although the spelling in some cases is phonetic, as for instance, 'Narroumershe. Tymber Hill is now South Parade and Gretesmythgate is Pelham Street.

There were 292 people named who between them contributed £50-6s-8d. Most of the payments are referred to as 'for his movables' the value of which would have been assessed whilst others were 'for his wages'. The lowest amount was 4 pence (4d) and 133 paid this sum. Only six people had to pay more than £1, the highest being £3 from Thomas Mellers, who lived on Low Pavement and £2-10s-0d for Robert Mellers on Gretesmythgate, both being bell founders.

A similar list was drawn up in 1643 when during the Civil War a committee of Parliament ordered the Mayor and Council to raise an assessment. A total of £540 was collected from 455, which indicated a considerable growth in population since 1524. Moreover, there were fourteen streets named which were not in the 1524 list. However, this throws some doubt as to the accuracy of the 1524 list as most of the new street names are to be found in the Borough Records up to 1484.

The amounts paid by the names in the 1643 assessment varied from a minimum of 6s-8d (6 shillings and 8 pennies) to £10. Only 'My Lady Grantham' was assessed at £10, and the Mayor and two Aldermen paid £5 each. The concentration of wealth on Long Row is shown by the fact of the sixty-three householders twenty-six paid £2 or more compared with the average of the town of £1-5s-0d.

TELEPHONE

In its issue of 1 January 1881, the *Nottingham Evening Post* had an announcement that the National Telephone Company was operating a telephone system in the town. The main exchange was in Thurland Street, with smaller ones on Derby Road, Mansfield Road and Nottingham Road. Calls cost 3d (three old pennies) for three minutes, with those to Long Eaton costing 6d (six old pennies). The first directory was published in 1885, when there were 180 subscribers. Most of those were business premises in the town centre, with a few private subscribers.

The directory gave instructions on the use of this new means of communication:

To call the operator signal by turning the crank briskly three times and wait until the operator rings your bell in reply, then take your telephone of the hook and listen. When you hear the operator's voice tell the number of the subscriber you wish to speak to and hang your telephone on the hook. When the bell rings again in reply it is the signal for you to converse. When you have finished talking, hang up your telephone and turn the crank again to signal the fact to the operator.

Subscribers were advised to press the telephone closely to the ear and converse quickly in an ordinary tone, about three inches from the transmitter:

Do not talk too loudly and be careful not to ring unnecessarily as this confuses the operator.

This example of an early telephone is in Brewhouse Yard's Museum of Nottingham Life.

In 1888 the system was expanded to enable calls to be made to other towns such as Derby, Leicester and some areas of Lancashire and Yorkshire.

The telephone service was later taken over by the government within the Post Office, until it was returned to private enterprise in recent times as British Telecom.

THEATRES

London had theatres for the performance of plays in Shakespeare's time, but it was 200 years until Nottingham had its first theatre. In 1760 the Theatre Royal was opened in a new building on St Mary's Gate and was often referred to by that name. According to the *Nottingham Date Book* part of the site had an earlier theatre but there are no other records of this.

The Theatre Royal had the County Hotel *on its left and a statue of Samuel Morley in front. Both have gone.*

Performances at the theatre were usually timed to take place when elections, horseraces and Goose Fair took place, ensured bigger attendances. They were mainly given by travelling companies of players including some from London. Abigail Gawthern in her diary covering the late eighteenth and early nineteenth centuries was a frequent visitor to the Theatre. On 12 August 1790 she recorded that she had seen Mrs Jordan in *The Country Girl* there. Dorothy Jordan was an Irish actress who had a successful career over thirty years. She also produced fifteen children, ten of them by the Duke of Clarence (later King William IV). The theatre closed in 1865 and was re-opened as the Alhambra Theatre, a music hall.

The present Theatre Royal was opened in September 1865 and was a venture by two brothers, William and John Lambert, who had a large textile business in Talbot Street. William became an alderman and a mayor of Nottingham. The programme on the opening night consisted of R B

Nottingham Playhouse has an added attraction in its skymirror.

Sheridan's *School for Scandal* and a farce entitled *Rendezvous.* Shakespeare's plays were performed, as were Gilbert and Sullivan's works, as well melodrama and comedies such as *Charley's Aunt.* Pantomimes were an annual feature starting with *The House that Jack Built* in 1865.

In more recent years, plays were often tried out at the Theatre Royal before being performed in London. The Empire Music Hall was built adjoining the Theatre in 1898. The latter was demolished in the 1960s and the site used for a new Concert Hall, the Theatre Royal being modernised at the same time.

One of the first cinemas to be built in Nottingham was the Goldsmith Street Picture Palace which, after the Second World War, became Nottingham Playhouse, a repertory theatre. The title was transferred in 1964 to a new purpose-built theatre on a site adjoining the Albert Hall. It was designed by a nationally renowned architectural practice, Peter Moro and Partners. Described in Pevsner's *Buildings of Nottinghamshire* as the only modern building of national importance in the City Centre, its design, both external and internal, contrasted sharply with the Theatre Royal, as do some of its productions.

THURLAND, THOMAS

Thomas Thurland was one of the seven original aldermen created under the Charter of 1449. He was also Mayor for that year and on seven further occasions. He was a merchant who became the wealthiest man in the town and contributed largely to the rebuilding of St Mary's Church. When he died he left a will of several pages in which he made many bequests to other churches and charities.

He had a mansion, Thurland Hall, which was later purchased by the Earl of Clare. This residence was chosen by monarchs on visits to the town as being more comfortable than the Castle. Clare Hall, as it became known, was demolished in 1831 and part of its site was named Thurland Street.

TOBACCO

Sir Walter Raleigh introduced tobacco into England in the sixteenth century and is commemorated in Nottingham by a street. It is rather curious that the name Raleigh is now connected with one of Nottingham's newer industries, cycle manufacture, whilst another such industry, tobacco, is commemorated by Player Street. This was in Radford near where John Player and Company's premises were built, a business started by John Player in the 1860s. *Pigot and Company's Directory* of 1828–29 listed four tobacco and snuff manufacturers. *Lascelles and Hagar's Directory* of 1848 listed six tobacco pipe manufacturers and twelve tobacconists, the latter including two manufacturers. So tobacco was well established in the town when John Player came to live in Nottingham in 1852. He was aged thirteen, the son of a Saffron Walden solicitor who had died a short time earlier. He started work at a shop on Long Row which later became Griffin and Spalding's (now Debenham's). He later opened his own business on Beastmarket Hill as agent for an agricultural seed and manure merchants. He also developed a sideline of selling tobacco

Player's tobacco factories provided work for both horses and motor vehicles.

in packets whereas previously it had been sold loose. This led to his concentrating on tobacco and in 1864 he was listed in *White's Directory* as one of sixty-eight tobacconists. In 1877 he purchased an existing tobacco factory in Broad Marsh, which made pipe and chewing tobacco and hand-made cigarettes. John Player died in 1884 shortly after he had built large factories at Radford. At first parts of these were used for lace manufacture, being let out to tenants.

John's two sons, John Dane and William Goodacre, later carried on the business when they were old enough and the firm, which had become a limited company, formed part of the Imperial Tobacco Group. The company and its trademarks became known worldwide and it was one of Nottingham's largest employers. Cigars and cigarettes were made in specially-built machines, supplementing the existing role of packaging pipe tobacco. The Radford offices were demolished in the 1990s and the new Horizon factory built on the edge of the City at Lenton.

From 1881, directories listed cigar manufacturers separately and in that year there were ten, one of which was Alton's on Derby Road. Their premises, which were in an elegant Georgian house, had the name painted on the brickwork. It has now been restored as living accommodation.

TRADE UNIONS

In 1792 James Tadwell and Peter Parker of Nottingham, cordwainers (shoemakers), were found guilty by a Grand Jury of:

> *combining and confederating with other journeymen cordwainers unlawfully to have their wages raised.*

Combinations were made illegal later by Acts of Parliament, until they were repealed in 1824. This resulted in a growth of trade unions, in Nottingham largely in the textile trades.

Lace manufacturers complained at a government enquiry that the men were so strongly organised that they had been able to have their wages raised to such an extent that some manufacturers had moved to Long Eaton where the wages were lower. On the other hand, the hosiery workers were more amenable to negotiating with their employers, which resulted in an Arbitration Committee being set up.

The increasing diversity of industry in the second half of the nineteenth century led to an upsurge in the number of trade unions such as those in the engineering, pharmaceutical and tobacco trades. The growth of the Labour Party in the twentieth century, when members obtained seats on the City Council, and at times a majority, led to greater co-operation between employers and workers. The rise and fall in the number of members of trade unions in the twentieth century nationally was reflected in Nottingham where the 'flight from industry' of the lace, hosiery and engineering and the replacement by leisure and service industries reduced the scope for the larger and more easily organised unions. Generally speaking, trade relations remain relatively peaceful as compared with more militant parts of the country.

TRAMWAYS
In 1872 the Borough Council's Highways Committee agreed that:

under proper and ample guarantees tramways may be laid down in such of the streets of the town as are wide enough to admit of them.

In November a draft agreement was approved for Nottingham Tramways Company Limited to lay down tramways. This required statutory permission and in 1874 the Nottingham Tramways Order was approved. This gave authority for two lines, one of which was only a single track. One was from St Peter's Square along Carrington Street then to the end of Station Street. The other line carried on from Carrington Street to the *Union Inn* on London Road. Workmen's fares were 2d (two old pennies) before 7 am and after 5.30 pm. Other lines followed.

The tramways were operated by a Company and were horse drawn. The steep Derby Road was too much for one horse and another horse had to be added from the Market Place. The agreement for public utilities run by companies provided that Councils could buy them after twenty-one years. Nottingham did so in 1897, after growing criticism that the system was inadequate for the growth of the town.

In 1894 the Council formed its electricity generating system and sent the City Engineer and the Electricity Engineer to the USA to report on electric trams there. As a result the Council decided to set up its own undertaking with power from overhead cables. An additional generating station was built, and stronger rails than those used for the horse trams were laid. An experiment using petrol driven omnibuses was not successful, although it proved its worth on one occasion when an electric power breakdown lasted all day.

An extensive system provided trams to all parts of the City and to some of the adjoining districts such as Arnold and Carlton. The increase in the number of automobiles on the roads led the Council to substitute trolleybuses on some routes, as these could pull up to kerbs, which trams could not. They were also powered by electricity and the last trams ran in 1936. Trolleybuses and petrol buses then operated until the 1960s when the trolleybuses were withdrawn.

☛ *See also Nottingham Express Transit*

TRENT BRIDGE

The Anglo-Saxon Chronicle was a written record of events in Britain from early Anglo-Saxon times and for some years after the Norman invasion. It records that in AD 920 King Edward the Elder captured Nottingham from the Danes and built a bridge across the River Trent. It was known as Heth Beth or High Bath bridge and became important in the growth of Nottingham as one of the few crossings of the River Trent. The original structure was of wood but later stone piers with cutwaters were added to the narrow arches.

It also became an important part of the town's property and one, which had to be maintained. Two bridge wardens were appointed and the earliest of their accounts which has survived is for the year 1458. This year was described as the one in which the bridges fell down for the want of repair and were repaired. The plural 'bridges' refers to the different arches of the bridge.

A chapel of St James had been built on the bridge and it became a source of income from alms. Some of the wealthier burgesses left property in their wills, the rents of which were to be used for maintenance of the bridge and these properties and their sites became quite valuable in later years. They were included in the Bridge Estate, which still survives with charitable status.

As early as 1838 the Council were aware of the need to re-build the bridge and started to accumulate funds from the estate for this purpose. In 1868, Marriott Ogle Tarbotton, who had been appointed as Borough Surveyor in

The many-arched bridge prevented river traffic of a passage beyond Nottingham.

1859, submitted a report on the need for a new bridge and forwarded designs he had drawn up. These were approved and the new bridge just to the east of the old one was opened in 1871. Because of increased road traffic it was doubled in width in 1925 and further alterations have been made in recent years at the south end of the bridge where one arch of the old bridge has been retained on an island site.

UNIVERSITIES

Nottingham has two universities. The first started life as the University College built by the Borough Council in 1881. A proposal to use the Castle for the College was turned down on the grounds that it was too far away from the town centre. It was eventually housed in a new building on Shakespeare Street, which also included a Free Library and a Natural History Museum. It was regarded at first as a University Extension of London University to provide classes locally for those unable to take up university residence. It soon became a notable feature of Nottingham's educational and cultural life.

Its future was assured by the erection of modern new buildings on land at Lenton, mainly due to the generosity of its benefactor, Lord Trent (then Sir Jesse Boot). It also had a School of Agriculture with premises at Sutton Bonnington and a Yarn and Textile Testing Bureau. The granting of the full status of University with the granting of its own degrees followed in 1948.

The university has grown since then physically with new buildings for science, the teaching hospital of Queens Medical Centre and in 1997 a new site, the Jubilee Campus. It has also played an increasing role of research and co-operation with industry.

The front of the original University College building has a richly decorated façade.

Apart from the Victoria Centre flats in the distance, all the buildings in the picture belong to Nottingham Trent University.

The Shakespeare Street building was taken over in 1946 to form Nottingham and District Technical College. New buildings were erected on Burton Street and Goldsmith Street. Clifton Hall became part of the college for teacher training and the title was changed to Trent Polytechnic and finally granted university status as Nottingham Trent University, including the former College of Art. Other new buildings in and around Shakespeare Street have led to a more or less complete campus.

VICTORIA BUILDINGS

Nottingham Corporation's decision to build flats for working class tenants started in 1875. It decided to build one block at Basford, near to the Gas Works, for employees there. Unfortunately, neither the gas workers or anyone else were enthusiastic about living there and after soul-searching they were demolished twenty-five years later.

At the same time it was decided to build another block of flats on Bath Street for Corporation workmen. A design by Arthur Nelson Bromley, a Nottingham architect, was accepted. The cost was £7,200 for ninety-three one, two and three bedroom flats in five storeys. Lifts were of course not even contemplated. The design include open-well staircases with buttresses adjoining. Within these buttresses were water closets, a modern innovation compared to the large number of privy middens in the town. The top toilet in each staircase had access from the flat roof. There was also a day room or common room and a resident caretaker was appointed. The Council decided before the flats were completed that they could be let to any one as well as corporation employees. The council were dissatisfied with the progress of the building work and threatened the contractors with financial penalties. The flats were completed in August 1877 and if the councillors thought that their hopes of providing good homes for poor families would be realised, their hopes were soon dashed. First of all numerous defects were found in the construction and the rents of 6/- (six shillings) per week had to be reduced to 5/- (five shillings) because tenants who had been used to paying rents of perhaps 3/9 (three shillings nine pennies) could not afford them. The tenants who could afford rents soon became a problem, the Council being unable to collect all the rents. The police regarded them as the worst dwellings in the town and by 1881 most of the flats were described as filthy and some were overcrowded.

As a result, the council handed the management to the Nottingham Town and County Social Guild. This body had been formed in 1875 for middle class ladies to carry out voluntary work to help the poorer classes to achieve better living conditions. They were organised in various branches, one of which including collecting rents. The first secretary was Miss Henrietta Carey and a member of the Council was Mrs Bowman Hart.

These intrepid ladies must have been astounded at the conditions of Victoria Buildings but did sterling work in getting rid of problem tenants, cleaning and disinfecting rooms and teaching the women tenants how to run a home.

The 1901 Census revealed that there were eighty-five flats but ten of them were unoccupied. Thirteen of the flats had only one living room. The number of occupants was 143, ninety-nine of whom were female and there were only thirteen children under ten years old. A hundred and seven of the occupants were working, mainly in manual occupations and often in lace and hosiery trades.

A hundred years after the building was erected, most of Nottingham's unfit houses had been demolished and the Council had built about 60,000 council houses since 1920. The Council conducted an inquiry as to the best way to deal with Victoria Buildings. Demolition was considered but dismissed. Instead some improvements were carried out making the flats into seventy-nine bed-sitting rooms and four lifts were installed. Despite this within ten years, tenants and social agencies complained about physical defects and environmental shortcomings, which were similar to those when the buildings were built.

This picture was taken in 1970 before the improvements were carried out.

The Council therefore decided to sell the buildings to a property company which carried out in 1990 a complete modernisation into eighty apartments, let on 199 years leases at prices from £30,000 to £39,000. Appropriately, the name was changed to Park View Court, as the apartments look out over Victoria Park, one of Nottingham's earliest recreation grounds.

Issues 96 to 100 (January 1995 to April 1996) of Nottingham Civic Society's *Newsletter* contain a five-part history of this building by Stephen Best, under the heading 'Minnitt's Folly'.

☛ *See also Farmer Family*

VICTORIA CENTRE

Fifty years ago Nottingham was described as 'still a Victorian City'. It certainly had a number of institutions with 'Victoria' as part of the title. One

A popular feature of the centre is Emmett's water feature, which springs into action on the hour.

of them was Victoria Station, which has disappeared, but in its place is Victoria Centre. This was Nottingham's first under-cover shopping mall. It was opened in 1969, the design and construction by Arthur Swift and Partners. The shops are on two levels, apart from a recent extra floor for one shop. Car parking was originally confined to the railway cutting. A bus station was at the north end originally but was moved further north, with open parking to make way for an extension of the shopping malls. Towering above are blocks of flats owned by the City Council. The Central Market was moved in to the Centre. The whole of the railway station was demolished, except for the clock tower, and the adjoining *Victoria Station Hotel* was retained with subsequent name changes.

VICTORIA EMBANKMENT
Of the many improvements which the Corporation carried out during the nineteenth century, one of the most imaginative was the decision in 1898 to construct the new road and embankment from Trent Bridge to Wilford. Its completion was a fitting start to the twentieth century. The start of the scheme at Trent Bridge was on what was known as the Old Waterworks estate and it was also necessary to purchase part of the land from the Clifton Estate. The ornamental gates at each end of the road were to signify that the road remained a private one owned by the Corporation. The scheme also ensured that the unbuilt on land to the west remained as open space as recreation grounds. Trees were planted along its length and give a pleasant outlook to travellers entering the City over Trent Bridge.

Subsequent additions included the Suspension Bridge, which also carried water mains to West Bridgford and in the 1920s the construction of the War Memorial and City pond and gardens behind it.

The western end of the embankment has a Wordsworthian display of daffodils in the spring.

One reason for building the embankment was the prevention of flooding from the River Trent. It did so with reasonable success until 1947 with the exceptionally severe winter causing flooding in much of the Meadows and West Bridgford. This was followed by a major reconstruction of the embankments on both sides of the river.

In the days when seaside and foreign holidays were for the wealthy classes, Victoria Embankment became a popular attraction at weekends and Bank Holidays. Regattas and swimming races in the River Trent are no longer held, but the summer months do see the venue used for festivals of various kinds.

VISITORS IMPRESSIONS

I cannot without lie or shame
Commend the town of Nottingham
The people and the fuel stink
The place is sordid as a sink

The medieval writer, believed to be a monk, perhaps from nearby Lenton, wisely remained anonymous. John Leland, writing about 1540, was more complimentary saying that the town had been well walled with stone with diverse gates, most of the wall then having been demolished. He had found it well-built with houses of timber and plaster on a climbing hill.

A hundred and fifty years later, Celia Fiennes said it was the neatest town she had ever seen 'built of stone and delicate large and long streets much like London and the houses lofty and well built'. She was perhaps favourably impressed by the cellars dug out of rocks. 'At the Crown Inn is a cellar of 60 steps down, where I drank good ale.' She was also 'very well entertained and very reasonably at the Blackmores Head'.

Five other visitors wrote of their impressions in the eighteenth century when the town was largely being re-built. Many of the new houses were of good quality and still remain, in such streets as Castle Gate and Low Pavement. The layout was particularly pleasant with gardens and orchards attached to them.

Most of these had been built on by the time J R Martin visited Nottingham on behalf of the Health of Towns Commission (see entry under that heading). Nevertheless it was not longer after his damning comments that Nottingham started to be referred to as 'The Queen of the Midlands'. No doubt whoever coined the phrase had not seen the whole of the town.

The transformation of the City in the second half of the twentieth century may not have resulted in eulogies of the kind Celia Fiennes used but the emergence of the City as a regional capital has been accompanied by an increasing trend for enterprises to relocate here.

WATER

A good supply of water was a prime necessity for the establishment of early settlements and Nottingham was fortunate in this respect as, apart from the River Trent, the porous sandstone on which the twin boroughs were built provided accessible wells.

The increasing population and urbanisation of the town meant that more organised methods of acquiring and supplying water were required. In January 1693 the Corporation agreed to get subscriptions to buy a water engine for the use of the town's inhabitants. In 1696 it was agreed that water should be brought into the town by pipes. A Waterworks Company was established to bring water from the River Leen, the Corporation taking four shares in the company.

The water was pumped from the River Leen to an open reservoir near the General Hospital from where it could be distributed by gravity. By 1827, the quality of the water had long been a source of complaint and the company erected a new Waterworks at Scotholme, Basford, although this still used water from the river, apparently from a point where it was not polluted. A rival company, the Northern Waterworks, was formed in 1827. This was fed from a deep well to a cistern, from where water carriers sold it at a farthing a bucket. Another company the Trent Waterworks opened a new works near Trent Bridge, taking water from the river to the reservoir at Park Row. The three companies amalgamated and in 1880, the Corporation bought the company out. It was already supplying some parishes outside the borough

The former offices of the Corporation's Water Department still have original decorative features.

and the Corporation continued to expand its area and built new works, including a pumping station at Papplewick, which is now an industrial monument. In 1912, the undertaking became a constituent of the Derwent Valley Water Board. The undertaking became profitable enough to hand over surpluses for the relief of City rates. In 1974 the Severn Trent Water Authority took over the various council and private undertakings in the area of its title.

WHITE'S LOAN MONEY

Sir Thomas White was an alderman of the City of London who as a merchant frequently visited various Midland towns. In 1553 he gave £1,400 to the Mayor and Corporation of Coventry to purchase an estate to provide funds for charitable purposes. One of these was what became known as the Coventry Money. The Coventry Corporation was one of five Midland boroughs, the others being Leicester, Northampton, Nottingham and Warwick, which were to receive £40 each every five years. This was to be used for making loans of £10 to four young men to start them in business. The loans were interest free and had to be repaid after nine years. Nottingham received its £40 every fifth year until 1692. In that year the other four towns discovered that Coventry had also improperly used themselves the profits of the estate, instead of distributing it in equal parts to all five towns. After considerable legal proceedings lasting eighteen years, the Courts decided that Coventry had held £2,241 over the years, which should have been shared. Nottingham and the other three towns received £212 as the legal costs reduced the £2,241.

From then onwards Nottingham continued to receive annual payments including profits starting with £405 in 1715 and rising to £674 in 1799. The charity is still available for making loans and has now quite considerable funds.

WINDMILLS

The elevated position of Forest Road, from where the land sloped northwards and southwards was a natural one for the building of windmills. The first mention of them appears to be in a minute of the Common Council in 1763. This stated that a committee of the Mayor, Aldermen and five other members of the Council should visit a site on the Forest to decide upon a suitable piece of ground for a Mr Inglesant to erect a windmill. A similar application in 1807 was approved at the risk and hazard of the applicant. The millers were allowed to build fences round them to prevent persons approaching within range of the sails.

In 1831 William Sharpe's mill was attacked and damaged by Reform Bill rioters and the Council allowed him £29 7s 11d compensation. There had been abut thirty windmills on the Forest and other high grounds, but these had all vanished by 1858, as steam powered mills took their place. One mill did, however, survive and this was at Sneinton, the home of George Green who became a famous mathematician.

The Mill became derelict for many years until it was restored and used as a factory for making polish. This ended in 1947 when the mill suffered a fire, which left it derelict again, although the brick structure remained. Some thirty years ago George Green's mathematics were found to be relevant to modern physics and admirers thought a fitting tribute to him would be the restoration of his former home. This proved no easy matter but eventually the mill was renovated and is once more grinding flour. A small science museum adjoining the mill has proved to be a popular attraction.

WILFORD

Today Wilford stands on the south bank of the River Trent, but until 1877 it was a parish, which extended across the river. North Wilford became part of the borough, those living south of the river no doubt pleased to have lost it, as it had a coalmine, which destroyed its tranquillity. There was a toll bridge over the river connecting the two parts, which replaced a ferry, which had seen fatal accidents. South Wilford, with its endowed school, retained its rural charm beloved by artists, poets and picture-postcard photographers. The coming of the Great Central Railway in 1900 did little to detract from its appearance, as there was no station.

In 1935 South Wilford, which had been governed since 1895 by Basford Rural District Council was transferred to West Bridgford Urban District. The part known as Wilford Hill was developed for housing but in 1952 the village of South Wilford west of the railway line was transferred to the City as part of the land purchase of the adjacent Clifton.

The garden centre at Wilford crossroads has gone, replaced by a public house and dwellings.

WIRELESS

The early 1920s saw the invention of wireless communication to broadcast news, educational programmes and entertainments to people in their own homes. The first sets were known as crystal sets with tuning by a device known as the 'cat's whisker'. Reception was at first through headphones but loud speakers soon became available. Nottingham had its own relay station, the service having the call sign 5GN, controlled from a studio in Bridlesmith Gate. Reception was via aerials fastened to large wooden poles usually some distance from the house. In 1922 the Estates Committee gave permission for tenants of council houses to erect such aerials in their gardens. By 1926, the Director of Education reported that sixteen City schools had wireless sets, mainly built by boys under instruction from teachers. This new science led to the profession of wireless engineers and to shops supplying sets and re-charging the lead acid accumulators. The extension of electricity to most houses resulted in the latter being rendered obsolete.

A company called Rediffusion introduced a system whereby subscribers could receive programmes by landlines connected to speakers for a weekly payment, thus alleviating the necessity to purchase a wireless set.

In the 1930s Nottingham City Police pioneered the use of wireless communication of police cars with headquarters. Broadcasting became an important medium of news and entertainment in the Second World War.

☛ *See also Radio and Television*

WOLLATON

Wollaton had three references in Domesday Book, each with a different spelling – Waletone, Olavestone and Ollavestone. These were all attempts at writing down 'Wulflaf's farm'. It is, however, a later landowner who was to transform *Waletone* in the sixteenth century. He was Sir Francis Willoughby who took his surname from the Nottinghamshire village near the Leicestershire border. He and Robert Smythson designed the ornate Wollaton Hall and laid out the surrounding parkland. The stone came from Ancaster and was paid for by coal from the Wollaton mine.

Wollaton was still partly agricultural and

The old centre of the village retains some of its historic past.

partly mining until the latter ceased in the twentieth century. In 1923 Nottingham City Council acquired the Hall and the parkland and built a housing estate mainly of bungalows, some of which were sold under a scheme whereby owners could pay the purchase price by weekly instalments.

Part of the estate was already on land within the City and the remainder together with the old village was in the county. This portion was brought into the City by an extension of boundaries in 1933. Much of Wollaton has been used for both private and council housing and remains mainly residential. The old village around the church retains its former aspect whilst the Hall and park are one of Nottingham's unique features, an Elizabethan Mansion, herds of deer and a golf course.

☛ *See also Workhouse; Guardians, Nottingham Board of*

YEOMANRY

White's Directory of 1853 reported that:

1794 was marked by the loyalty of the inhabitants of the town and county, in support of that constitution which Englishmen so much admire : four troops of yeomanry cavalry were raised out of the most respectable inhabitants.

The Riding School near the entrance to the Castle was demolished when the new Drill Hall on Derby Road was built in 1911. Its use has since changed, becoming residences owned by a Housing Association

The *Nottingham Date Book* noted that on 3 October of that year the Gentlemen Yeomanry of the Town Troop had a grand field day. There were sixty-seven of them and their captain, Ichabod Wright, gave them a sumptuous entertainment at Thurland Hall.

Yeomanry Cavalry troops were formed to assist the regular army should they be needed and were inspired by the feeling of unrest arising from the French Revolution. The Nottinghamshire contingent consisted of four troops and the Nottingham troop was:

decidedly the best appointed and most effective, the men being young and light and the horses handsome and active.

They were called into action in September 1801 together with Bunny and Holme Pierrepont troops when corn riots against the high price of flour broke out in Nottingham. They were used by the magistrates to escort supplies from the villages to the millers and generally to keep the peace.

It was from these early beginnings that the South Notts Hussars and the Sherwood Rangers were formed and played a prominent part in the two wars of the twentieth century.